Rational Investment

Why System Trading
is the Only Rational Way
to Invest

MARK I. LEE

ISBN: 0615604374
ISBN-13: 9780615604374

TO
KAY

TABLE OF CONTENTS

PREFACE

The motivation for this book lies in the hope of laying the foundation for a more rational, scientific approach to investing. Investors are subject to significant obstacles, many of which come from within. Far from the rational agent model of traditional economics, people tend to be quite irrational in their investment decisions. Further, the market itself is not as clear-cut and simple as many would have us believe; it has a life of its own, one that is complex and dynamic. Without a proper understanding of the underlying, any derivative strategies are doomed to failure. Profitable investing, then, involves strategies built on the assumptions of the market as it really is, not the way it is presented in economics textbooks.

The purpose of this book is to provide a rationale for the quantitative method of investing called *system trading*. In proving its efficacy, the fallacies of other, more common forms of investment are exposed—namely, discretionary investments, where the investor or trader trades on a whim or one-off idea continually, with no predetermined method and, hence, no justification for the validity of that method. System trading is a general method of investing that can be used in virtually any market.

One benefit of system trading's quantitative nature is that it easily incorporates the latest and greatest from the scientific world. Indeed, artificial intelligence technologies have been used widely, if sporadically, throughout the industry for over twenty years now. Further, software firms such as Ward Systems, along with the multiple third-party vendors for TradeStation and Interactive Brokers, have made these technologies widely accessible.

The first part of the book addresses the cognitive biases found within that hamper attempts at rational decision making. Ironically, these biases form part of the rich, diverse, and complex interaction of forces that make the markets so chaotic. The second part of the book presents the market as a complex adaptive system. As a system, a market is not merely chaotic; it is complex and capable of self-organization. The author draws heavily from complexity theory.

The third part addresses system trading. After discussing the justification for system trading's validity and its superiority over discretionary investing, the chapter details critical issues for successful system trading. Although still theoretical in nature, this chapter is the book's most practical, providing examples of walk-forward backtesting and an adaptive trading system. The book finishes with a genetic algorithm-assisted, fully adaptive trading system.

Partly because it lays out its claims in a falsifiable format to begin with, system trading is the only valid way to invest. It also provides a host of advantages over more common styles of investing. However, psychological resistance to it is surprisingly strong and persistent. Even traders with quantitative backgrounds (people comfortable with numbers) find the prospect of trading something as complex as the market with something as mechanical as a trading system inadequate at best and laughable at worst. After fifteen years of training, teaching, and arguing about the rationale and merits of system trading to traders, managers, and clients, the author has come to suspect that the hesitation is largely psychological. It goes deep down into our fears of reductionism and addressing difficult and uncomfortable phenomena without the aid of common crutches.

In the face of uncertainty, people want to know *why,* regardless of whether the answer will help them or not. Further, in the search for those answers, people would rather cling to simplistic models that make sense and make them feel comfortable. To be sure, consistent profits in the markets will not be had so easily. Until coming face-to-face with the harsh, often brutal, realities of randomness and uncertainty in the markets, an investor will remain imprisoned by the forces of fear and greed and remain forever lost and confused.

It is my hope this book will shed some light on these common points of confusion and offer a path to knowledge and consistent investment profits.

PART I: IRRATIONALITY OF INVESTORS

CHAPTER 1. FEAR, GREED, AND EXCITEMENT

Contrary to what economists may believe, investors are a highly irrational lot. They buy when they should sell and sell when they should buy. They bet small when the odds are in their favor and bet too much when statistics show they have a small chance for gain. This departure from rational models of behavior will be examined in greater detail in the next chapter. However, it is useful to begin by discussing the emotional forces driving investing behavior. Much of the irrational behavior in the markets is based on the emotions of fear and greed. This chapter will examine these two emotions and the kinds of irrational investment behaviors that arise from them.

The first point to clarify about emotions is that they are neither right nor wrong, rational nor irrational. It is the action we take based on emotion that make our *decision-making processes* rational or irrational. If an investment strategy tells an investor to buy this property, but the investor is full of fear because this is has been a "bad month," he or she is simply a fearful investor. That is normal and generally beneficial: it is fear that keeps us alert and careful. However, if the investor then decides not to buy due to this fear, he or she has made a mistake. The investor's decision-making process is irrational.

FEAR

Fear of the known is difficult enough to deal with; fear of the unknown can wreak havoc on one's reasoning and performance abilities. The degree of uncertainty found in the market is considerable. Hence, the fear investors exhibit throughout the investing process is understandable. It is a very real phenomenon, persistent throughout all markets. Experienced traders are very familiar with the effects and manifestations in market patterns of traders' fear. Some successful traders are able to capitalize on these patterns consistently.

A November 2010 *Wall Street Journal* article[1] discussed the rapid growth of the VIX[2]; it is estimated to have generated $25 million in fees for the CBOE, attesting to its popularity. Many note the recent increase as related to the general financial malaise beginning with the subprime crisis. However, a quick glance at a historical chart shows that the VIX has had many such spikes over the past twenty years (August 1998 and September 2002 had historic highs).

Another fear-induced pattern is the difference between the slope of uptrends and that of downtrends. Downtrends tend to move faster than uptrends in the equities,

---

1 Brendan Conway,. "Investing in Fear Is Big Business," *Wall Street Journal* (New York), 2010. Retrieved December 12, 2010, from http://online.wsj.com/article /SB10001424052748703785704575642643319238142.html
2 The volatility index is traded on the CBOE and is a derivative (futures) contract of the implied volatility of S&P 500 options. Because these options are often used as hedges for equity investors, it is often referred to as the "fear index."

whereas the opposite is true for commodities markets. Fear is considered a stronger emotion than hope. One can see the fear of long-only equity investors exiting the market en masse in fast downtrends.

In the same way, a supply shortage inspires fear and causes strong, quick spikes in commodities markets. Coffee grows close to the ground and is always in danger of frost, which can wipe out an entire season's crop. Hence, the mere rumor of frost will drive commercials to buy futures, as reflected in several quick spikes to historical levels throughout the past four decades. The subsequent move back down was much more protracted.

Dow Jones Industrial Average (2004-2009)

Fear can manifest itself in subtle ways. Unable to cope with the uncertainties presented by the markets and investing, investors often seek explanations where there are none to satisfy a desperate need for certainty. Because of the complex, self-organized nature of the markets, answers for *why* the market moved a certain way are largely absent. In spite of industry hypothesizing and the media's constant speculations, causes are far too numerous, dynamic, and nebulous to identify.

Coffee Futures (1972–2009)

In fact, this need to know the causes is so strong, investors often invent reasons for which there is no evidence. These are called superstitions. One of the main manifestations of fear in investors is a need to be *sure* about their investment. Superstitions tend to manifest themselves most strongly *when they are fearful*. Superstitions also tend to abound in areas of people's lives in which there is strong pressure to perform, such as sports. Unfortunately, investors have a special list of superstitions that have persisted, despite abundant evidence that they are not rational.

COMMON INVESTMENT SUPERSTITIONS

— The All-Powerful Federal Reserve—Many investors hold to the myth that the government, the Federal Reserve, the "insiders" (i.e., one special group of powerful people), control the markets. It is comforting to believe that the government can make the markets go up to assuage our fear of losses. But consider: if the Fed had that much power, why would the markets *ever* go down? They would just buy every time the markets started declining. The fact is, the market is far too big for any one group or cartel to control.

— Political events—Every time the market makes a dramatic move, newspapers write titillating copy to entice readers to their pages. Most of the time they get the details wrong, and the reasoning is always flawed. There is never *one* reason the market surged 2 percent on a particular day. For example, this is the headline from www.marketwatch.com (January 20, 2010): "The (US) stock market hit a new 15-month high Tuesday, spurred by the biggest jump in health-care shares since the summer as traders bet on the outcome of a Senate race with big implications for proposed health-insurance reforms." In truth, the market had been going up for some time. Do people spend an inordinate amount of time reading the news, seeking an explanation for why the stock market is going down? Or why the economy is bad? When investors are feeling confident, they rarely look for explanations.

— Options expiration/triple witching days—It is amazing how experienced traders continue to fear this event, as if it had some mystical power over their positions. However, the size of market movements caused by options expiration or multiple witching days is greatly exaggerated. First, how many traders really wait for an event that occurs on a regular basis and that everyone knows about? The truth is, most investors will take action on their positions in the days leading up to the expiration day. Second, the markets of today are very liquid. With more advanced electronic exchanges (e.g., CME Globex) and algorithmic trading capabilities, volatility during this period has been greatly minimized. In most cases, it will not be the reason investors lose or win money that day.

— Here is a random list of superstitions the author has heard over the years from within the investment industry:
  — Don't talk about a winning position; it will get rid of your good luck.
  — Make sure your trading desk has good feng shui.
  — There are some markets that fit your personality and some that do not (W. D. Gann, the legendary trader, has been known to have said that there are markets some traders will never make money in because it doesn't fit the trader).
  — The market is crashing; maybe if I sacrifice stock A, the rest of my stocks will do well.
  — Never put a stop-loss on an even number price.
  — As soon as I buy this stock I know the market gods will punish me by dropping the stock.

To reiterate, the existence of fear is not bad; it is healthy and beneficial. Being overcome by fear and making bad decisions based on fear (not facts or sound reasoning) is the basis of irrational investing.

GREED

Warren Buffet once said, "We simply attempt to be fearful when others are greedy and to be greedy only when others are fearful"(Warren Buffett, 2001). Goldman Sachs strives to be "long-term greedy." In truth, an investor should never act out of emotion or psychological motivation. All investment acts should be taken in the search of monetary profit based on objective assessments of risk and return.

Greed can be defined as an inordinate desire to possess more than one needs. In investing, greed is the emotional need to go beyond the limits of (1) realistic performance and (2) the natural limits of the investment itself.

Although a full book can be written about what can be considered good investment performance, most have wildly unrealistic expectations. The top hedge funds in the United States average 15–20 percent returns after fees. The reason they are the top funds is because they have been able to do this on a consistent basis for over ten years. Further, "consistent" does not mean 15 percent every year. If one looks through their returns, one will see that they all have great years, where they make 50+ percent, and bad years, where they lose -10+ percent. Averaging 15–20 percent on a yearly basis for many years will make one an extremely wealth investor.

Many times investors will try to stretch or "overperform" their investment strategy or vehicle's realistic expected return. It would be like asking your bank for 7 percent interest on a short-term CD, when the Fed overnight rate is at 2 percent. Often greed is the flip side of fear. Missing investment opportunities out of fear makes one greedy in subsequent trades as a reaction to catch up or grab the ones that got away.

One common manifestation is betting too much. Any complete investment strategy must have a component that tells investors how much to risk in each investment. When investors get greedy, they *randomly* increase this amount. If one believes the win probability of this particular investment is greater, one should simply adjust his or her strategy. But one isolated increase in the risked amount is a clear sign of greed.

This greed-inspired increase in risked amount is one of the reasons volume swells toward the end of a trend. It is also the reason markets get volatile during this phase. And it is the reason so much money changes hands when the trend reverses.

Markets are generally designed to lure traders into the market. Market makers and brokers only get paid if a trade takes place. Market makers employ a variety of techniques to cause trades to occur, such as quick spikes on news releases. Many of these trades are knee-jerk reactions inspired by the prospect of a quick profit. Brokers are a crafty lot as well. Any seasoned investor has fielded numerous sales calls from hungry brokers looking to meet their quotas to make their Christmas bonus. Make no mistake, these brokers use all manner of tactics to lure investors into making trades they normally would not have made.

THE NEED FOR EXCITEMENT

The most common reaction to initiates of system trading is, "It's boring!" This type of rational and disciplined trading is not for most people. It is repetitive and, hence, requires the trader to relinquish what draws many traders to the markets in the first place: freedom and creativity. Because of the inherently uncertain nature of the market, traders are free to create whatever they see fit and have the freedom to trade as they wish. Where's the fun in simply placing orders and monitoring your positions? There's no excitement of "going with the flow" of the market. It is too rigid. It is missing that element of surprise. These are the same people who say the "market is my hobby," "it is my lover," "my inquiry into the nature of the universe...." Even experienced traders, who have been knocked around the market enough to know it is not a "hobby" to be treated lightly, succumb to this temptation from time to time.

At some point in an investor's career, he or she will have to face the question: do I want money or _____ (insert the many temptations of the market)? Ed Seykota, a legendary trend-follower, once remarked, "Win or lose, everybody gets what they want out of the market. Some people seem to like to lose, so they win by losing money." There is evidence that seeking excitement is dangerous and, hence, should be avoided.

Marvin Zuckerman of the University of Delaware has been studying personality traits in the context of risk-taking for over twenty years. He invented the Sensation Seeking Scale to delineate and rate the degree of sensation seeking in various personalities. Zuckerman has found that sensation seekers tend to estimate risks as being lower, even when they have no prior experience in the activity.[3]

One of the very real dangers is caused by skilled scalpers looking to capitalize on traders looking for excitement. Market-makers in exchange-traded markets will spike the market up, only to bring it down over the next few minutes. What's going on here is that there are sell orders that need to be filled. To get good prices, market-makers need to entice traders to come in and buy their sell orders at higher prices.

How do they entice them? By spiking the market up. A sharp move up in the market gets traders excited. In the US markets, this type of manipulation has become common-place, especially during news releases. Traders waiting for news, asking for economic report results, are invariably novices who still believe that news moves the markets. Once a report comes out, markets get volatile and sucker in these traders. In the worst case, markets will break out of a consolidated range to the upside before reversing and starting a longer-term downtrend. More often, a trader will buy into this type of situation in an excited state, then get out when prices reverse quickly. Excited traders will quickly go from greed to fear and back again.

---

3 Marvin Zuckerman, "Sensation seeking and risky behavior," *American Psychological Association* (2007): xix.

CHAPTER 2. COGNITIVE BIASES

WHAT IS RATIONALITY?

The concept of human rationality was built by the labor of celebrated philosophers, scientists, and economists over the past two thousand years. We have spent the past few decades deconstructing this edifice. Recent work in cognitive theory has struck a serious blow to its foundations. Human rationality exists, but it is far more difficult to make rational decisions than we thought.

Rationality is the result of combining some utility function with a logically integrated system or model to optimize that utility function. To deviate from this system or to behave in a manner inconsistent with one's specified goal would be considered irrational. Working toward a goal without a logically integrated system would lack rationality as well.

Wolfgang Welsch is much more articulate:

> 1) We speak of rationality whenever people follow a specific set of principles which determine the realm of their validity, identify their objectives, define the aims to be achieved, the methods to be followed, and the criteria to be applied. 2) These principles must be coherent with one another in order to allow coherent usage. 3) Therefore, to be rational simply means to follow the rules suggested by these principles.[4]

In other words, one can speak of a system of actions as rational or irrational. What is required for such a system to be rational is the pursuit of a utility function, or objective, in a systematic manner, where said system is logically valid and coherent. In the context of investment, the utility function is investment profit or risk-adjusted profit. The system would be the trading method or strategy with all the necessary parts to meet the objective. This method should be clearly spelled out so that it can be tested for efficacy (i.e., it actually meets the objective). It also needs to be clearly defined, so that its internal logic is shown to be valid.

In sum, a rational investment method must meet the following requirements:

1) Testable: all necessary and sufficient rules within system are clearly defined and integrated coherently
2) Clear objective of profit maximization
3) Evidence of efficacy: evidence that it is profitable (meets its objective)
4) Logical validity: methods and core components must be logically valid

---

4 Wolfgang Welsch, *Rationality and Reason Today*, eds. Dane R. Gordon and Józef Niznik (Amsterdam: Criticism and Defense of Rationality in Contemporary Philosophy, 1998).

Most endeavors of any significance do not meet the above requirements. It is not because people are unintelligent. As the world becomes more complicated, available choices often overwhelm decision makers. Forces of evolution have honed quick decision-making skills. These are called heuristics; they are quick rules of thumb that have made us faster and smarter. In fact, they are part of our natural evolution as a successful species.[5] Indeed, the latter part of this book discusses the power of artificial intelligence technologies, many of which are built on simple heuristics.

Where complication meets complexity is where random, uncertain phenomena come into play. Markets have a perceivable order, but the uncertainty of future prices creates risk. Such uncertainty arises because the dynamics are unclear. They are numerous, they change, and their interactions create more chaos. In such situations, quick thinking begets bad outcomes. Although our heuristics have allowed us to master everyday events of surprising complication, they are woefully inadequate to address complexity on any scale. In such situations, a different kind of analysis is necessary—one of a more deliberate, extensional, and statistical nature. The use of heuristics in such complex situations creates cognitive biases.

There are many known cognitive biases. The branch of finance that deals specifically with this area is called *behavioral finance*. Its founders are largely recognized as Daniel Kahneman and Amos Tversky. Other notable figures include Richard Thaler and Thomas Gilovich. Daniel Kahneman won the 2002 Nobel Prize in economics for his work in prospect theory. Numerous cognitive biases have been identified, and recognizing them is key to investment success. Every time a bias sneaks into an investor's decision, his or her returns are likely to suffer.

TRUST YOUR GUT

"Trust your instincts." Investors are given this advice with alarming frequency. Even professional money managers take pride in their gut. Tversky and Kahneman are sympathetic: "Because we normally do not have adequate formal models for computing the probabilities of such events [events involving uncertainty], intuitive judgment is often the only practical method for assessing uncertainty."[6]

However, behavioral finance has shown that decisions made from the gut are highly prone to error. Trusting your intuition leads to the many cognitive biases depending on the specific decision that is to be made. Something as risk-laden as investing surely requires careful deductive reasoning involving statistics and probability. Unfortunately, without the proper decision frameworks and sophisticated decision-making tools in

---

5 Gerd Gigerenzer and Peter M. Todd, *Simple Heuristics that Make Us Smart* (New York: Oxford University Press, 1999).

6 Amos Tversky and Daniel Kahneman, "Extensional versus Intuitive Reasoning: The Conjunction Fallacy in Probability Judgment," *Psychological Review* (1984).

place, even professional managers default to their intuition. Two of the most fundamental cognitive biases are representativeness and availability biases.

REPRESENTATIVENESS AND RECENCY (AVAILABILITY) BIAS

Probability is a well-defined part of mathematics; to calculate the probability of a future event, there are very specific steps and clear formulas. Instead of calculating the probabilities, an investor with representativeness bias (RB) will simply ask whether this event seems *like* other events he or she has seen before. More often than not, the investor will simply recognize an event that is similar to something seen elsewhere and conclude, often incorrectly, that the outcome will be the same.

What Tversky and Kahneman were able to show was that these two types of judgments are of different kinds—probability being extensional and representativeness coming from the intuition. Hence, we often find ourselves engaged in the wrong kind of thinking. When we see a man running out of a bank wearing a ski mask, the assumption might be that he is a bank robber. What we are doing is using the ski mask and the running to represent the activity of robbing. If we met someone big, our immediate reaction might be to be intimidated, associating size with aggression.

David Hardman has written an excellent textbook called *Judgment and Decision Making—Psychological Perspectives,*[7] in which he writes extensively on cognitive biases in a much more detailed and formal manner. He explains RB in terms of a prototype heuristic, whereby the prototype is the representative exemplar and is used to represent a category. The prototype is "judged by the degree to which the individual resembles (is *representative* of) the category stereotype."[8]

Hardman points to a study conducted by Desvourges et al. (1993), where it was found that the amount people were willing to donate to save endangered birds in an oil spill was unrelated to the number of birds. The average amount for saving 2,000 birds was $80 and the $88 for 200,000 birds. "The explanation in terms of prototype heuristics is that people create a prototypical instance, such as an image of a bird drowning in oil, in order to represent the deaths of numerous birds. This image creates an emotional response that is then mapped onto a monetary scale."[9]

Another common way that RB manifests itself is the base rate fallacy, where one makes a snap judgment about the prevalence of an event without taking into consideration the actual probability (prior probability) of that event. Instead of calculating the base rate, one focuses on similarities between events that may look similar but are

---

7 David Hardman, *Judgment and Decision Making—Psychological Perspectives* (London: British Psychological Society and Blackwell Publishing, Ltd., 2009).
8 Ibid.
9 Ibid.

different in kind. In the size example above, one should consider the base rate of big people who are actually aggressive.

This cognitive bias is one of the main reasons discretionary investing is so troublesome. Everyone has a favorite indicator (e.g., Thursday jobless data for bond traders, Andrew's pitchfork for technical traders). There is nothing wrong with the efficacy of that particular indicator. The mistake is taking one instance where it worked and generalizing it as a trading strategy. Often, that one indicator was seen as the reason for a spectacularly successful trade and is subsequently seen as the *cause* of successful trading. Doing the research and finding the base rate would be the right way to do it. Often, one finds that the indicator works far less often than one originally thought.

Another more egregious mistake people make in the investment industry is the misperception of random events. One of the human mind's greatest skills is pattern recognition; this is one area in which it is far superior to computers. As a result, we often see patterns where none actually exist. Some of this misperception is superstitious in nature, stemming from our need for explanation; and some of it comes from RB.

RB is also one of the main reasons for failures in executing successful trend-following systems. A simple look through the backtest of a trend-following system (the majority of them have similar performance statistics) might reveal that it has had several periods of six consecutive losses or more. Trend-following systems typically have low win percentages but make their profits in their outsized win:loss ratios. Even a 50/50 coin toss of over 1,000 would hit on a twelve-consecutive run of either heads or tails. These events are primarily due to the random nature of the markets, rather than the lack of efficacy in the trend-following system. However, many traders give up on the system after a few consecutive losses, incorrectly judging that the system is broken.

Many of these cognitive heuristics are so deeply engrained, it takes a great deal of effort on a daily basis to avoid biases. Even after fifteen years as a professional trader, the author hears the call of Recency Bias (ReB) frequently. ReB weights the more recent information more, even though all relevant information should be considered. At Rational Investment Research, the author manages a portfolio of intraday systems, which trades more frequently than most trading systems. Within the same week, RIR's portfolio can feel superb after a few days of consecutive wins and seem downright awful after a few days of consecutive losses. Of course, the feelings are never acted upon, but they are there; and without the proper experience, skill set, and technology, it is understandable why so many fall prey to ReB.

ReB is part of a larger bias called the *Serial Position Effect*. The Serial Position Effect, coined by Hermann Ebbinghaus, describes the varying accuracy of memory recall based on the position of the memory in the subject's entire list of memories. Thus, ReB is the tendency people have to weight recent memories more strongly than distant memories. So an investor with ReB who recently had a string of losses might start to doubt his investment strategy. Instead, he should examine the entire list of trades and judge his performance objectively. System traders have the advantage of a backtest to use as an objective measure. More advanced system traders have more sophisticated methods of continual monitoring, evaluation, and validation of their strategies.

ReB is one instance of a general class of biases associated with the availability heuristic. Again, Tversky and Kahneman were the first to identify this heuristic.

Investors are said to employ the availability heuristic whenever they estimate frequency or probability by the ease with which instances or associations could be brought to mind. To assess availability, it is not necessary to perform the actual operations of retrieval or construction. It suffices to assess the ease with which these operations could be performed, much as the difficulty of a puzzle or mathematical problem can be assessed without considering specific solutions.[10]

Hardman makes a useful distinction between "recall of content versus ease of retrieval."[11] He points to a study by Schwarz et al. (1991), where more people who were asked to recall six examples of assertive behavior rated themselves as assertive than people who were asked to recall twelve examples.

ANCHORING

Anchoring occurs when individuals need to make an estimate without context (e.g., what will be the high of crude oil today?). People will come up with an initial guess, the anchor (e.g., yesterday's high, say $55.00), and then make upward or downward adjustments to the anchor based on additional information. The anchor is subjective and is generated because the decision maker cannot recall the exact datum. In some cases, this anchor becomes the assumption upon which an entire argument or research program is built. Further, decision makers often adjust too much or too little away from this anchor. They then come to rely too heavily on this anchor and make subsequent decisions with a strong bias toward that value.

Anchors are often derived from irrelevant sources. Currency traders are prone to focus on double-digit numbers as support and resistance levels (e.g., 1.3100). The second problem is that individuals will continue to use this anchor when it is no longer warranted. Markets will trend for some time and then abruptly reverse, or range for a while and then rapidly breakout into a trend. Traders with anchors at specific prices cannot adjust to the new change and continue in their old trading habits, using their anchors as reference points.

For example, a trader buys a stock and it hits a new high at $20, causing him or her to exit at a profit. At that price the trader is likely to anchor that stock's price to that new high. It then reverses back down to $15, and the trader buys again, believing that it will go back up to $20 as it did before. As it continues to decline, he or she will stubbornly hope that it will eventually go back to the anchor price. What does not occur to the

---

10 Amos Tversky and Daniel Kahneman, "Judgment under Uncertainty: Heuristics and Biases," *Science* (1974).

11 David Hardman, *Judgment and Decision Making—Psychological Perspectives* (London: British Psychological Society and Blackwell Publishing, Ltd., 2009)

trader is that the market is in a new downtrend, and he or she should be forecasting lower prices.

As Hardman points out, anchoring may be due to a phenomenon called *selective accessibility*. When presented with a question that compares one value to another, the data is selectively accessed in subsequent discussions. Mussweiler and Strack (1999) go further and suggest that decision makers using the anchoring heuristic answer comparative questions "by testing the hypothesis that the target's value is *equal* to the anchor."[12]

For example, traders may be asked what they think the price of gold will be a year from now without any reference points. Or the question can be phrased, "Do you think gold will be higher or lower than $1,000/oz a year from now?" When asked in a comparative manner, traders are likely to anchor their responses to the $1,000 and continue selectively accessing this price from memory over any other price. They then proceed to compare future price discussions and ask whether that price is equal to $1,000.

Further, Wilson et al. (1996) found that decision makers with greater domain knowledge are less susceptible to anchoring bias, because they are able to filter out irrelevant data and thus decrease the instances of anchoring to the wrong data points. If one has been trading gold for twenty years, one knows that gold can be quite cyclical, and that anything over $500 is quite rare.

HINDSIGHT BIAS

Any proprietary trader with more than a few years' experience has a number of war stories. The author once worked for an interesting division manager inside a large securities firm. During down equity markets, he would routinely call his main equity traders after the market close and grill them using the day's price chart, asking why they did not buy here and sell here. No discussion ever occurred before the market, and there were no clear decision frameworks in place. Egregiously bad management to be sure, but lesser forms of hindsight bias persist throughout the industry.

Hindsight bias is a phenomenon where "an uncertain outcome…seems more likely *after* it is known that the outcome has occurred."[13] This bias is relatively well-known: "hindsight is always 20/20." Discretionary forms of investment are especially prone to hindsight bias due to the lack of clear evaluation measures. An investor can easily say he made that investment because he knew that chart pattern would work or the new administration's economic policies would benefit the economy. There is no way to verify if that was the reason for the investment decision initially. In addition, because there is no data to prove the causal relationship, an investor could also claim he was right, even if the outcome was the complete opposite (e.g., "I knew the new economic policies would tank the market!").

---

12 Ibid.

13 Ibid.

There are three main schools of thought on why hindsight bias occurs:

1) The motivational approach—decision makers are motivated to preserve their self-esteem or reputation by making their predictions more accurate
2) The memory impairment approach—when the outcome becomes known, it immediately alters or hinders (make less accessible) the original memory trace
3) The biased reconstruction approach—decision makers forget or never made the original decision, and, in the absence of that decision, it is replaced with an anchor based on the outcome

Researchers believe that the biased reconstruction approach starts with a biased sampling of outcome-related images in the memory. The memory is then reconstructed using such images. Thus, "the set of images retrieved during reconstruction most likely differs in a systematic way from the set of images retrieved during the generation of the original estimate (decision). As a consequence, the reconstructed estimate (decision) will most likely be biased towards the solution (outcome)."[14]

David Aronson holds the position that a subjective (discretionary) approach to technical analysis is doomed to hindsight bias, from which there is no remedy other than taking an objective approach to technical analysis:

> I contend that hindsight bias is unavoidable because it is impossible to shield oneself from the outcome knowledge. Simply knowing the path that prices took biases the analyst's perception of the predictive power of whatever method is being evaluated. Only objective TA (technical analysis) methods offer the opportunity of avoiding hindsight bias because only information known at a given point in time is used to generate signals, and signals are evaluated in an objective manner.

Indeed, numerous studies have shown that hindsight bias is exhibited even in cases where participants were informed about the phenomenon. Aronson's prescription is clear and one that all serious investors must heed:

> subjective analysts could protect themselves from hindsight bias if they were willing to make falsifiable forecasts. A forecast is falsifiable if, at the time a forecast is made, the analyst specifies (1) outcomes that would constitute a forecast error, or (2) the procedure that will be used to evaluate the forecast as well as when the procedure will be employed.[15]

---

14 Rudiger Pohl, *Cognitive Illusions: a Handbook on Fallacies and Biases in Thinking, Judgement and Memory* (London: Psychology Press, 2005).

15 David Aronson, *Evidence-Based Technical Analysis* (Hoboken, NJ: Wiley, 2007).

OVERCONFIDENCE

> In 1984, *The Economist* asked four European former finance ministers, four
> chairs of multinational firms, four Oxford students, and four London gar-
> bage collectors to predict the next decade's inflation, growth rates, and
> sterling exchange rates. Adding up scores ten years later, the garbage
> hauliers [sic] tied the company bosses for first place, and the finance min-
> isters finished last. (Myers, 2002, p. 158)[16]

So far, it has been shown that the greatest enemy an investor can face is often him- or
herself. It is not ignorance or lack of intelligence, but rather a systematic psychological
scheme of error that prevents sound decision making. But it gets worse. Not only do we
have a host of forces sabotaging sound judgment, but these cognitive biases are also
often hidden or shrunk from our view—so much so that we are also plagued by a class
of overconfidence biases as well. The evidence is clear that we believe we are better
decision makers than we really are.

As a group, these biases are called *attribution biases*. They affect our reasoning for
why something happened (i.e., to what we attribute the outcome of our decisions).
Sometimes called the *overconfidence effect*, overconfidence bias (OB) is one of the best-
documented cognitive biases. People with OB have greater confidence in their judgments than their actual accuracy would warrant. Many specific attribution biases, especially the ones discussed below, contribute to OB. These biases as a whole lead investors
to incorrect conclusions, because they identify the wrong causes.

OB exists when two components do not match: confidence level and objective accuracy. In an ideal world, an investor would have a 65 percent confidence level that
his investment would succeed, and he would be right (make a profit) 65 percent of the
time. In other words, he would have a clear sense of his accuracy level, if not a clearly
defined range of probability.

However, most people's confidence levels far exceed their objective accuracy. Stuart
Oskamp tested clinical psychologists on questions related to a case study. They were
also asked to provide a confidence rating to their answers, so that a comparison could
be made between the subjects' confidence levels and the accuracy of their answers. The
interesting thing Oskamp did was to provide more information about the case to help
the subjects. As they were given more and more information, their confidence levels
increased from 33 percent to 53 percent. However, as they were given more information, their accuracy did not improve significantly, remaining below 30 percent. Note that
these were professionals. By and large, professionals in the medical, legal, and investment areas exhibit OB to an alarming degree.

Many behavioral finance researchers have found that overconfidence causes traders
to trade much more frequently than traders without OB, even though their overall re-

---

16 Ibid.

turns are at or below relevant benchmarks. Apparently most traders believe that their trading skills are good enough that trading more will produce more profits. This study and the Oskamp study also point to another specific bias that causes people not only to become more confident with more information, but also to actively *seek out* information so that they may feel more confident. This bias is called the *confirmation bias*.

CONFIRMATION BIAS (CB)

Confirmation bias (CB) is a tendency people have to selectively collect information that supports a preconceived notion and neglect information that negates that notion. An investor with CB, who believes stock A is going up, will look for positive news about stock A, seek other investors who believe stock A will go up, or talk with a broker who is selling stock A. At the same time, the investor will actively avoid information that says stock A will go down.

In many institutional trading departments, particularly those trading stocks, consensus building is heavily employed. If trading involves a securities department, the research departments are pulled in as well. The investment decision process is not one of objective analysis, whereby viable choices are evaluated against a preexisting model or framework and then invalidated because they do not meet the conditions; instead, subjective choices are confirmed with a variety of fundamental and technical factors. In the end, the quality of the decision is severely impaired, and consistent losses are perpetuated.

The basic mechanism by which this bias is acted out is selective collection of new evidence as opposed to a complete examination of all relevant information. For example, in many studies subjects were found to frame questions in such a way as to provide the answers that confirm their existing beliefs.[17] Subjects conducted one-sided "research,"—neglecting to search for evidence that would falsify their belief—and stopped as soon as they found information that confirmed their belief.

The scientific method was designed to weed out errors of this kind. It seeks to *negate* hypotheses instead of simply trying to *validate* them. CB causes people to do the exact opposite—investors tend to use any bit of information they can simply to confirm their hypothesis rather than to contradict or adjust it.

When conflicting evidence is encountered, it creates cognitive dissonance. Someone with CB finds different ways to ease this dissonance. One subtle way is by applying double standards. "The standard applied to evidence that supports a favored position is the gentle requirement that it have a ring of plausibility or the possibility of being valid. In

---

17 Raymond S. Nickerson, "Confirmation Bias; A Ubiquitous Phenomenon in Many Guises," *Review of General Psychology* (1998).

contrast, the standard applied to evidence that conflicts with cherished beliefs is that it must be *convincing beyond any possible doubt.*"[18]

The superstitious employ this technique regularly: "For believers in faith healing (for example), a colorful corroborating account is accepted without question. However, a controlled scientific study denying the efficacy of faith healing would be faulted on any and every possible ground, reasonable or otherwise. By demanding that dissonant evidence be so strong that it be compelling beyond any doubt, while only requiring that harmonious evidence be weakly consistent, holders of erroneous beliefs are able to keep their faith alive."[19]

Herein lies another weakness of discretionary, fundamental investing. Because, in most cases, there is no preexisting framework or set of conditions with which to *negate* an investment opportunity, it leads most investors to commit CB. Because there is no framework by which to judge whether the new information supports the initial choice or an alternative, the investor intuitively selects that which confirms his or her initial belief. In system trading or other quantitative-based trading strategies, CB creeps in with less frequency and magnitude. The clearly defined entry and exit rules negate initial overconfidence.

To be sure, there are investors who employ fundamental analysis in a rational manner and profit consistently from it. However, many novice investors start with no model or framework and use a collection of unrelated facts to reach a decision. Individual pieces of information are not systematically integrated with each other. A model or framework would help integrate and organize the facts, so that logical inconsistencies would be clarified, and complementary facts would be integrated to calculate probability profiles. Without adherence to rational models, investing often becomes an exercise in increasing confidence in a decision that has already been made.

This process is employed by discretionary technical analysts as well—many of whom add indicator after indicator to a chart. Highly correlated indicators add nothing of value to the analysis process; in fact, they often increase what statisticians call *overfitting.* Overfitting is like cherry-picking the best examples from the past to make the analysis appear more accurate than it really is.

SELF-ATTRIBUTION BIAS (SAB)

"Heads I win, tails it's chance." (Langer and Roth, 1979)
Self-attribution bias (SAB) is one of the primary causes of OB. SAB is the human tendency to attribute positive outcomes to their abilities while attributing failures to external circumstances. In investments, investors will attribute wins to their skills and losses to other events or people. Even a bad strategy will win a few times. In fact, if one flips a

18 David Aronson, *Evidence-Based Technical Analysis* (Hoboken, NJ: Wiley, 2007).
19 Ibid.

coin 1,000 times, one will get a consecutive series of twelve heads or tails. Thus, chance can generate a successful series of wins, regardless of an investor's skill. When this string of wins occurs, the investor attributes this success to his or her foresight, special knowledge, or skill instead of chance, thereby becoming overconfident.

One example in the financial industry is the "psychological call option," for which investors use financial advisors. Many investors take advice from financial advisors. Often when the investment is successful, the investor will take the credit it for it, attributing the success to his or her skill. If the investment is a failure, the investor has the option to "protect his ego and lower his regret by blaming the advisor."[20]

It is likely that some of the headline-grabbing lawsuits and bailouts over the past few years fall under this category. SAB caused investors to rationalize failure by blaming everyone but themselves for a voluntary decision. Investment losses were blamed on the government, the economy, a friend's bad advice, or a broker.

Thus, instead of accepting failure, learning from it, and evolving to perform better next time, many investors rationalize failures and doom themselves to repeating the same mistakes. Such investors have learned absolutely nothing about investments and have not improved their investing skills. But the investors' perceptions of their skill levels have been magnified. Even worse, overconfidence may lead them to increase their bets or venture into other areas, of which they have no knowledge.

To some degree, SAB originates from an investor's inability to face the harsh truths of the investing business and take full responsibility for his or her actions. However, taking full responsibility is one the keys to success. Robert Prechter, CEO of Elliott Wave International, had this to say about the importance of taking responsibility for mistakes one makes while investing:

> Accept responsibility. There are many evasions of responsibility that automatically disqualify millions of people from joining the ranks of successful speculators. For instance, to moan that "pools," "manipulators," "insiders," "they," "the big boys," "program trading" or Fed chairman are to blame for one's losses is a common fault. Anyone who utters such a conviction is doomed before he starts....Take every gain and loss as your due, and you will retain control of your ultimate success to the extent that the market will allow.[21]

The most telling aspect of this fallacy is that the average person, upon sitting down and thinking it through thoroughly and clearly, would see the logical mistakes. Indeed, as discussed briefly in the introduction, biases arise because the intuition is employed when reasoning is needed. Most people do not want to undertake the arduous process

20 Thorsten Hens and Kremena Bachmann, *Behavioural Finance for Private Banking* (Hoboken, NJ: Wiley, 2009).
21 Robert Prechter, *Prechter's Perspective* (Atlanta: New Classics Library, 1996).

of reasoning, calculating, and analyzing. If one does make this effort consistently, one will make money investing.

ILLUSORY CORRELATION (IC)

Illusory correlation (IC) is the tendency to mistake a coincidence for a correlation to fit one's preconceptions. During 2007–08, leading up to the subprime crisis, the crude oil market was hitting new highs every month. During that time it was noted in the news on a daily basis that the rising cost of crude oil was the main reason for dips in the stock market. The justification was that higher oil prices would increase costs for companies, thereby lowering profits. However, a simple look at the long-term charts of both the crude oil and S&P markets would show that if anything, they move in the same direction. Indeed, a year later, the same media outlets were saying exactly the opposite of what they had reported: crude oil going up shows increased demand in the economy, and stocks should go up.

These kinds of ICs are rampant in the media. But the correlation simply does not exist. Establishing the correlation between two set of data is a tricky business and requires a significant knowledge of and experience in statistical modeling. In one study by Redelmeir and Tversky (1996), symptoms of arthritic patients were recorded along with weather conditions over a fifteen-month period. Almost every patient recorded that their symptoms were directly linked to weather conditions. However, scientific studies have concluded that there is no relationship between the two.

In both examples above, arbitrary factors that do not increase the predictive accuracy of the investor's judgment are added indiscriminately. If each new bit of information was differentiated, non-correlated to the existing factors, and this new bit of information supported the hypothesis, increased confidence may be justified. But a positive jobs report, a strong assessment by the President's economic team, and a bullish report by a leading economist on the labor market should not increase investors' confidence that the economy is doing well—at least not any more than just one positive jobs report. In technical analysis, it does not help to add a stochastic to an RSI indicator, as they both measure price gains and losses (although the precise formulas are different).

This bias is the cause of fundamentals-based investing's greatest myths: the stock market is correlated to the economy. That is, a good economy will cause the stock market to go up, and a bad economy will cause the stock market to go down. This myth is unsubstantiated—there is no evidence of this correlation. It is illusory and will get a fuller treatment in the section on Irrational Markets.

OVERCONFIDENCE SUMMARY

The three specific biases mentioned above—confirmation bias, self-attribution bias, and illusory correlation—are the main causes of overconfidence bias. It is critical to identify these biases in one's decision-making processes. According to many researchers, Wall Street analysts have an average forecast error of 44 percent. Many other professionals, including doctors and lawyers, commit overconfidence bias regularly as well. If trained, experienced professionals make bad decisions due to overconfidence bias, it must be taken quite seriously.

Stated more strongly, unless one's investment strategy is built on a model or framework that is *quantifiable and measurable*, one is likely succumb to overconfidence bias, to one's detriment. The objective nature of system trading makes it far superior to both fundamental-based and technical-based discretionary trading. The key components are clearly defined and falsifiable.

Compare the two following predictions:

1) The S&P 500 will be higher over the long term.
2) There is a 40 percent chance that the S&P 500 will increase 10 percent over the next three months.

The first statement can be true or false on the same day, depending on who said it. The second will either be true or false but not both. It is falsifiable and allows for an objective assessment of predictive ability. An investor with a strategy built on statements like the second is in good shape. In the worst case, if a prediction turns out to be wrong, the investor will know exactly why and will have a good idea of how to improve. Moreover, the investor will be making rational investment decisions, free of cognitive biases.

CHAPTER 3. PROSPECT THEORY

EXPECTED VALUE THEORY

Cognitive biases are deviations from a normative model (i.e., a rational model of decision making). When it comes to making decisions involving risk and reward, such as investing, the expected value theory or model (EVM) is the standard model. Simply, the optimal choice among options involving risk of loss and possibility of gain is calculated by weighting (multiplying) the value of the outcomes with the possibility of their occurrence. In other words, one should multiply how much one stands to gain by the probability of the outcome. The result is the expected value, and the choice with the highest expected value should be chosen.

System traders calculate the expectancy of a trading system in a similar manner. Expectancy is usually calculated thus:

*Expectancy = (Average Win * Probability of Win) - (Average Loss * Probability of Loss)*

As an example, a trend-following system wins 30 percent of the time. It makes, on average, $1,000 when it wins, and loses, on average, $300 the 70 percent of the time it loses. This system's expectancy would be

*($1,000 * 0.30) - ($300 * 0.70) = $90*

Many traders have a hard time with trend-following systems because of their low win percentage and high win:loss ratios. Losing several times in a row can be difficult on the ego, and making 10–15 percent returns on one single trade can be more stressful than one thinks. However, according to the EVM, the correct decision is to trade this system, as it has a positive expectancy.

The EVM sounds obvious, but most forms of investing do not make this simple calculation. In fact, most forms of investing cannot even be formulated thus, because the two variables cannot be quantified. Indeed, much of what investors do deviates from basic rational decision-making models. Even before that consideration takes place, cognitive biases warp decision makers' objective view of risk and reward, such that deviations from EVM are the norm.

EVM is restrictive in many real-world contexts, as shown by Bernoulli's famous St. Petersburg paradox. Thus, expected utility theory (EUT) was proposed as a better, more flexible normative model of decision making that replaces the expected value with a utility function that varies with the decision maker. As long as investors maximize the chosen utility function, they are considered rational.

Unfortunately, traditional economics has taken EUT as a descriptive model and applied it widely. In their original 1979 paper,[22] Daniel Kahneman and Amos Tversky critiqued the EUT and proposed a more realistic model, representing the irrational thought processes of decision makers. This theory is called *prospect theory*, for which Kahneman won the Nobel Prize (Amos Tversky passed away before the prize was awarded).

PROSPECT THEORY, OR HOW PEOPLE *ACTUALLY* TAKE RISKS

Through a series of hypothetical, two-outcome gambles, Kahneman and Tversky showed that there are three main ways that EUT fails as a descriptive model. These patterns were confirmed by the responses of students and faculty. First, although EUT suggests risk aversion, Kahneman and Tversky developed a fourfold pattern of risk attitudes (FFP) that differed depending on the outcome (gains or losses) and whether the probabilities associated with the outcomes were big or small.

In the first problem, participants had to choose between the following options[23]:

Problem 1a:	A. Certain gain of 3,000	B. 80 percent chance to win 4,000 or nothing

The expected value of B is 3,200, which is more than choice A. However, 80 percent of the participants chose A. This finding conforms to EUT, as it is *risk-averse*. However, when offered another version of the same problem but with losses instead of gains, anomalies start to arise:

Problem 1b:	A. Certain loss of -3,000	B. 80% chance to lose 4,000 or nothing

The expected value is lower for choice B, that is, it is the riskier option. Ninety-two percent chose B; hence, participants in the face of losses were *risk-seeking*. The next two problems were similar, except that the probabilities for gains and losses were very small.

Problem 2a:	A. Certain gain of 5	B. 0.001 chance to win 5,000 or nothing
Problem 2b:	A. Certain loss of -5	B. 0.001 chance to lose 5,000 or nothing

For Problem 2a, 72 percent chose B, whereas for Problem 2b, 83 percent chose A. Thus, when probabilities are small, participants were risk-seeking for gains and risk-averse for losses.

---

22 Daniel Kahneman and Amos Tversky, "Prospect Theory: An Analysis of Decision Under Risk," *Econometrica* (1979).

23 Examples are taken from Hardman, p. 67–69

In sum, the FFP states that individuals are (1) risk-seeking over low-probability gains, such as buying lottery tickets; (2) risk-averse over high-probability gains, such as not buying insurance; (3) risk-averse over low-probability losses; and (4) risk-seeking over high probability losses, such as casino games. Therefore, the EUT's implication that decision makers are risk-averse is untrue; in the real world, risk attitudes vary according size, gains/losses, and probabilities.

The second problem with EUT is that decision makers typically do not calculate the outcome utilities by their probabilities. In fact, "people overweight outcomes that are considered certain, relative to outcomes which are merely probable."[24] This problem was originally discovered by another Nobel-prize winner, Maurice Allais, in a 1953 *Econometrica* paper.

EUT can be expressed mathematically as a utility function, most commonly as

$$U(x)=-\exp(-aW)$$

where W is wealth and a is the relative risk aversion coefficient. Using this formula on two separate experiments should yield a similar outcome. However, participants in the Kahneman and Tversky study violated two different outcomes that could not result using this formula.

In Problem 1, participants were offered

A1:	2,400 with certainty	B1:	2,500 with probability of 33 percent
	2,400 with probability of 66 percent		
	0 with probability of 1 percent		

and 82 percent chose B1. However, in Problem 2, when offered

A2:	2,400 with probability of 34 percent	B2:	2,500 with probability of 33 percent
	0 with probability of 66 percent		0 with probability of 67 percent

Eighty-three percent of the participants chose A2. A utility function, like the one above, would choose either A1 and A2 or B1 and B2. However, participants chose B1 and A2, violating the EUT.

In Problem 1, the following decision was made:

$$1(a2,400) > 0.66(a2,400) + 0.33(a2,500) + 0$$

Reformulated for comparison, 0.66(a2400) is subtracted from both sides[25], and the third term is eliminated, resulting in the following:

---

24 Ibid.

25 Ibid.

$$0.34(a2,500) > 0.33(a2,500)$$

In Problem 2, the following decision was made:

$$0.34(a2,500) < 0.33(a2,500)$$

In essence, subtracting a common term in Problem 1 makes it the same as Problem 2. An axiom of EUT, known as *Savage's sure-thing principle*, states that preferences should be determined on factors that are *different*. In this example, participants' decisions were affected by an attribute that was the same in both problems.

Kahneman and Tversky observed more closely the phenomenon where participants were risk-averse for gains and risk-seeking for losses when the outcomes are identical. They called this the *reflection effect*.

In another experiment, participants were given 1,000 and then asked to choose between

A.   50 percent chance of gaining 1,000   B.   Certain gain of 500

and to choose between the following after being given 2,000

C.   50 percent chance of losing 1,000   D.   Certain loss of 500

The majority of participants chose B and C. However, A and C are identical when the participant's assets are taken into consideration:

A = 1,000 + (1,000 * 0.50) = 1,500
C = 2,000 - (1,000*0.50) = 1,500

Of course, B and D are also similar when asset outcome is accounted for:

B = 1,000 + 500 = 1,500
D = 2,000 - 500 = 1,500

Participants are unable to incorporate their assets into their calculations and isolate the outcomes from the entire calculation. This phenomenon was referred to as the *isolation effect*. This miscalculation is part of an overall phenomenon Kahneman and Tversky identified as coding, where participants "perceive outcomes as gains and losses, rather than as final states of wealth or welfare."[26]

Kahneman and Tversky were able to develop a model that captures the dynamic of the FFP, such that it can predict the behavior of decision makers in risk-taking situa-

---

26 Ibid.

tions. Prospects, or the gambles represented in the problems above, are chosen in irrational ways inconsistent with the EUT. Prospect theory (PT) accounts for this irrational decision making, providing an excellent descriptive model for how risk-reward decisions are made in the real world.

PT models decision making in two phases: editing and evaluation. In the first phase, editing, participants reformulate the options so as to simplify the choice they have to make. The coding phenomenon mentioned above is one of the operations participants undertake, which effectively cuts short the total calculation of gains to wealth. Cancellation is another operation participants employ to create the isolation effect. Through cancellation, participants "discard the components that are shared by the offered prospects."[27] Many of the cognitive biases outlined by Kahneman and Tversky in subsequent research occur during this editing phase. Once the editing is complete, each prospect is evaluated for the highest value.

In the evaluation phase, a formula, consisting of a value and weighting function, models participants' choices in prospects.

$$U = \sum_{i=1}^{n} w(pi)v(x_i) = w(p_1)v(x_1) + w(p_2)v(x_2) + \ldots + w(p_n)v(x_n)$$

where x_1, x_2 are the potential outcomes and p_1, p_2 their respective probabilities; w is the weight and v is the value. The value function, $v(x)$, represents the subjective value of the outcome. Generally, participants tend to value outcomes relative to some reference point. The value function measures the deviation from that reference point.

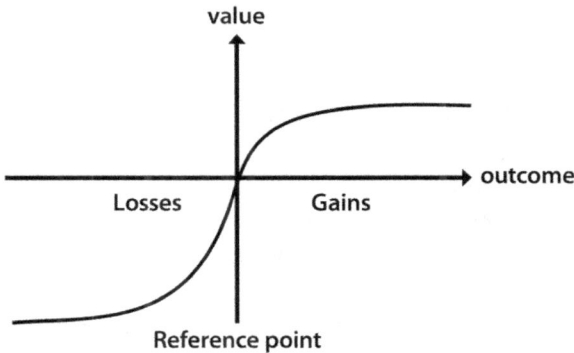

value

Losses   Gains   outcome

Reference point

There are two important features of this value function. Based on empirical data from the experiments discussed above, the value function tends to look like a S-curve that deviates from the reference point in greater magnitude for losses than for gains. In other words, a loss of $100 is felt greater (as reflected in subjective value) than a gain of $100. Also, the curve is also concave for gains and convex for losses, representing greater sen-

---

27 Ibid.

sitivity to changes near the reference point and less sensitivity as changes get further from the reference point. In other words, initial losses and gains are felt more sharply than subsequent losses and gains of the same amount.

Weighting of probabilities is the other key component of PT. It is represents the over- and underweighting of probabilities in different scenarios by decision makers. The second problem discussed above indicated that participants had overweighted certain probabilities over lesser probabilities. Also, small probabilities affect preference choices greatly, and the weighting function allows PT to account for this influence.

APPLICATIONS

PT is arguably the most successful model of human decision making, able to account for the major factors in risk-taking decisions. As such, PT has a wide range of applications, especially in finance. The simplest lesson it teaches investors is to avoid these kinds of deviations from rational decision making by calculating the expectancy of investments and have the discipline to choose and follow the course of action that maximizes utility.

Another general pattern of behavior PT highlights is the tendency people have to underweight outcomes that are merely probable in comparison with outcomes that are obtained with certainty. However, investing is not an exercise in certainty; the bigger the returns, the bigger the risk. Any well-developed market with easy access (e.g., equity markets, exchange-traded products) will invite a tremendous amount of competition. In chapter 4, the complex nature of the market will be examined in detail; for now, suffice it to say that markets can only function by becoming complex and making it supremely difficult for traders to extract gains. Hence, to be a successful investor, one must learn to be comfortable with uncertainty and must have a method of investment that accounts for this, using the sophisticated methods of statistical analysis.

A more specific and formal application of PT is what is known as the disposition effect (DE). DE is the tendency for investors to hold on to losing investments longer than winning investments; investors tend to sell winning investments much faster. This tendency is likely due to the greater sensitivity investors have toward losses than gains. Further, investors also tend to gamble more (i.e. make low probability bets) to recover those losses.

Profitable trend-followers do the exact opposite: they cut losses short and ride out gains. Further, researchers have shown that the stocks investors sell tend to go on to greater gains on average than the stocks they decide to hold on to (Odean, 1998). That is, if the investors had held on to those stocks they decided to sell, they would have made more profits. If they had sold the losing stocks (i.e., cutting losses), they would have cut short their losses, thereby contributing to greater overall gains in their portfolio.

PT also explains why trend-following strategies are so difficult to accept and, if accepted, to execute properly. Holding on patiently as long positions continue to make profits can be more stressful than expected. Many investors become acutely sensitive to any corrections and will continue to feel tempted to close out the position. Outright rejection of trend-following strategies for "safer" arbitrage or counter-trend strategies is common as well. With a higher win percentage, loss aversion is maintained, and investors can lull themselves into a false sense of security. However, countertrend strategies have an "option short" profile, where losses are rare but large. When the big losses eventually come, even valid strategies are discarded, as the loss aversion continues its hold on the investor.

PART II: THE IRRATIONALITY OF THE MARKETS

CHAPTER 4. COMPLEXITY THEORY
AND THE MARKETS

INTRODUCTION

Behavioral finance's historical significance may very well come from exposing the fundamental problems of traditional economics. However, it is far from a normative model of the economy, much less the markets. Complexity theory offers a solution to a fundamental misunderstanding of the markets and has provided numerous, if disparate, models of market behavior. Far from the rational, efficient model proposed by the Efficient Market Hypothesis (EMH), the market is a swirling mess of chaos whose primary feature seems to be uncertainty. It turns out, however, that the market is not so easily dismissed. Amid the chaos, periods of quiet, steady order and organization appear, seemingly out of nowhere. At "the edge of chaos"[28] lies complexity, a condition exhibiting both randomness and order. Thus, it appears that the market is best seen as a complex adaptive system (CAS).

This chapter starts with some basic considerations of what a market is, then moves on to a discussion of the basics of complexity theory, ending with alternative models of market behavior supported by our previous discussion of cognitive biases and the basics of complexity theory.

To start from scratch, what is the main goal of a market? Think about it for a moment. The market's goal is not to make everyone rich. It seems more often that the market is trying to make everyone poor. Some participants willingly lose money in the market to obtain some other goal (hedgers). To provide a place for buyers and sellers to transact in an orderly and efficient manner is probably as good a goal as any.

Consider for a moment what a good market would look like. What would a bad market look like? If a market exists as a place to provide buyers and sellers, a good one would attract more such traders. Greater diversity would allow for larger numbers of trades. Providing for a different class of traders would diversify it further. After all, if everyone is after the best prices, relative value functions are the only trades that would actually take place.

To attract traders with different goals, a good market would provide incentives to speculators—speculators of all types, scalpers, long-term position traders. It would attract gamblers with action until they cannot gamble anymore, and it would provide investors who need to get out quickly with ready buyers. It would attract hungry market makers to get the whole thing started.

What exactly does a market gain by adding all these layers of complication? The more traders, the greater the diversity of their objectives, the more liquidity provided to all

---

28 Christopher G. Langton, "Computation at the edge of chaos," *Physica D* (1990): 42.

participants. Hence, the market's main job is to provide liquidity. This creation of liquidity is circular and builds on itself with a continuous feedback mechanism—one of the hallmarks of CASs. Not providing liquidity would make it a poor market. To the extent that it is liquid, it would be judged a good market. Hence, the market will do everything it can to provide maximum liquidity to its participants. Currently, investors are blessed with some of the best markets man has ever seen.

The past few years have witnessed a plethora of failed investment types and strategies, such as "stat arb," the yen carry trade. Although numerous dynamics are involved, one valid way to look at these failures is to see the market adapting to tight liquidity constraints in one sector by "freeing up" that liquidity.

Freeing up this liquidity means moving money from one trader to another. Of course, the first is losing money, while the second is profiting. Unfortunately for the bulk of investors, a free market's profits are asymmetrically distributed: 10 percent gain from the 90 percent of losers. Thus, many are led to feel that markets should provide less certainty. However, a good market will do everything it can to *increase uncertainty* in a market, so that no one strategy has the advantage over another; as Edgar Peters put it, "Uncertainty is the market's main source of *stability* and *innovation*."[29]

The way a market optimizes itself, that is, maximizes liquidity, is by organizing itself into a CAS. On the one hand, it must maintain order and some measure of stability to attract speculators and other traders who rely on predictability. On the other hand, it must maintain a measure of risk and uncertainty, changing forms, patterns, and other broad characteristics, so that no one participant can manipulate the market, thereby restricting liquidity.

Due to the *decentralized nature* of a CAS, it can generate an enormous amount of complexity at all levels, confounding all manner of skilled traders from short-term, high-frequency traders to long-term position traders. Indeed, the market is a thing unto itself—the result of the interaction between hordes of traders who compete and cooperate with each other—the dynamics of which are best understand with complexity theory.

WHAT IS A COMPLEX ADAPTIVE SYSTEM (CAS)?

In *Complexity: The Emerging Science at the Edge of Order and Chaos*, M. Mitchell Waldrop describes a complex adaptive system as having the ability to balance order and chaos, existing at *the edge of chaos*. Here, "life has enough stability to sustain itself and enough creativity to deserve the name of life. The edge of chaos is where new ideas and innovative genotypes are forever nibbling away at the edges of the status quo, and where even the most entrenched old guard will eventually be overthrown."[30]

---

29 Edgar E. Peters, *Complexity, Risk, and Financial Markets* (Hoboken, NJ: Wiley, 2001).
30 Mitchell M. Waldrop, *Complexity: The Emerging Science at the Edge of Order and Chaos* (New York: Simon and Schuster, 1992.<<what year?>>).

Waldrop generalizes four characteristics of a CAS: (1) complexity, (2) spontaneous self-organization, (3) adaptability, and (4) dynamism. Other key concepts of complexity theory include emergence, loose coupling, randomness, decentralization, and evolution. Rather than being a specialized science, complexity theory is more a general field of inquiry drawing broad concepts from many different fields. Its success can be measured in the numerous specialized sciences it has spawned or inspired, such as genetic algorithms (artificial intelligence) and biological paradigms.

COMPLEX

A CAS is *complex* in the sense that it derives its power from a vast number of agents interacting with each other, rather than a few big agents impacting its environment directly. A typical CAS is composed of individual agents, nonthinking automatons that are usually very limited in their abilities. But the great number of these simple agents interacting with each other in unfettered ways can create surprisingly sophisticated behavior. All of these interactions can go both ways and also morph into other interactions, such that it is impossible to isolate individual actions.

Think of the fifty billion neurons in the human brain and how they are all connected to each other in one vast network. As Holland points out, a typical neuron has a fanout (the number of direct connections to other neurons) ranging from one to ten thousand; comparable connections in modern computers have fanouts of less than ten. The difference between the two is roughly three orders of magnitude, which is "enough to call for a new science."[8]

Just as billions of neurons are networked together to form the brain, thousands of traders are networked together to form a market. What generates complexity is that there are no prescribed rules of cooperation or competition. No one tells the agents to act together or against each other. Those dynamics emerge unpredictably as a result of their interactions and the constraints they face at the system level.

Moreover, the interactions that connect each agent to others go both ways. This non-linearity is central to CASs and creates a rich, dense complex structure, one that is very different from the linear relationships we are more accustomed to in our everyday lives. We are used to the simple, classical physics paradigm where throwing a ball will make it go away from us. But imagine how complex our lives would get if the ball could throw us as well. Further, numerous feedback loops are created within the system that feed on itself simply due to its structure. This feature allows systems to "remember" and reinforce certain behaviors. Negative feedback allows the system to absorb changes from its environment, leading to stability, whereas positive feedback amplifies changes, leading to instability.

Without feedback mechanisms, the world would be vastly simpler. Indeed, as Miller and Page astutely point out, ignoring feedback mechanisms have allowed economists to avoid the complex real-world dynamics of economies and markets: "[I]f agents either avoid direct interaction with one another or interact in such a way that strong negative feedback results in a stable equilibrium"[⊠] the world would be much easier to understand. The Efficient Market Hypothesis is roughly a model of market behavior absent the positive feedback that Brian Arthur has so arduously articulated throughout the years.

SPONTANEOUS SELF-ORGANIZATION

As agents find ways to cooperate and compete, "the very richness of these interactions allows the system as a whole to undergo *spontaneous self-organization*."[⊠] Nobody tells the myriad traders of the EUR/USD currency market to cooperate and buy to create an uptrend. Governments would love to have this power and raise the stock market to infinity. But trends, ranges, and all kinds of market patterns organize themselves, a result of the interactions between cooperating and competing traders. Below, the spontaneous part of "spontaneous self-organization" will be discussed further, as patterns tend to appear rather abruptly.

One of the most fascinating aspects of a CAS is its ability to create "order for free,"[⊠] Stuart Kauffman's famous term denoting the natural and spontaneous way a CAS orders itself.[⊠] We are so accustomed to thinking of organization as a result of some higher intelligence. We attribute the order found in nature to intelligent design. Yet, complexity science has been able to provide a whole new paradigm to view the order we see around us, and that order is wholly endogenous to itself.

One of the market models discussed below explains the specific mechanism behind trend formation that is wholly self-organized. Positive feedback loops in complex systems are another way a CAS organizes itself without exogenous help.

ADAPTIVE

Many solutions for the problems that arise from our environment tend to be of the static, simple kind. Successful policy changes by the government that become fixed in the legal code often become dated and prohibitive as the environment changes. One way to frame this problem is to see a policy change as an organism that is tailor-made to thrive in the current environment. It is so tailored to that environment that, if static and rigid in its structure, it becomes a victim of its own success; when the environment provides different constraints, it cannot cope—and dies.

CASs have a decentralized structure that gives them maximum flexibility, allowing each CAS to try out many different solutions to continually seek out the optimal solution as the environment around it changes. This adaptability gives CASs a long-term stability that allows them to continue on, even as more static structures around them die out. Thus, its loose, chaotic structure becomes one of its biggest assets. For example, the greater number and level of diversification a market has, the greater its ability to decentralize and create complexity; this structure then allows it to survive, neutralizing influences from large traders and government interventions.

John Holland and John Miller, both key researchers in complexity theory, almost euphemistically point out the static, overly simplistic approach of traditional economics: "Economic analysis has largely avoided questions about the way in which economic agents make choices when confronted by a perpetually novel and evolving world."[31] People are used to applying static concepts and models to the market. It is comforting and easy to look for and devise simple rules, guidelines, and principles that should somehow always hold true. However, the markets, like the economy and most things in the natural world, are in constant flux.

Specific agents within a larger CAS also contribute to a CAS's ability to adapt. Anecdotal evidence suggests that only 10 percent of traders are consistently profitable. By continually adapting to changing market conditions and also by learning from mistakes, these profitable traders become better,[32] more profitable traders. Their trading capital continues to grow and contributes to the overall capital available to the market, thereby increasing market liquidity. Rather than switching back and forth between two less skilled traders and feeding brokers in transaction costs, who then take that capital out of the market, a skilled trader becomes a source of liquidity to the market.

Most traders learn from their experience to some degree, but they learn much more from other traders, especially in the early stages. Highly skilled traders draw knowledge from other fields, such as artificial intelligence and behavioral finance. This transmission of knowledge in the form of successful strategies and techniques is spread and adopted by traders through a variety of communication channels within and on the periphery of the market. This process is exactly what genetic algorithms do to evolve solutions, mimicking biological processes. Thus, the market ensures its continued evolution through adaptive traders.

DYNAMISM

Waldrop describes the fourth characteristic of a CAS as a dynamism that is neither chaotic nor static. The parts that make up a CAS interact in many random ways, but they also create order spontaneously. Part of the reason for this complex interaction is that they interact *with* each other. That is, most of us are used to the arrow of impact or

---

31 John H. Holland and John H. Miller, "Artificial Adaptive Agents in Economic Theory," *The American Economic Review* (1991).

32 There are many definitions of good performance. Here the author refers to the general class of risk-adjusted performance measures (e.g., Calmar, Sharpe ratios) with which to judge a trader's ability.

causality going in one direction. However, within a CAS, the arrow moves in many directions, and agents act upon each other after being acted upon.

Thus, this dynamism is what distinguishes the merely complicated from the complex. A ball of yarn is complicated, but it is not complex. There are a specific number of strings—usually just one—and the strings do not change or interact with one another. If one takes the time to untangle the string, one can simplify the "system." Such phenomena are not complex, because the strings do not change one another.

Large corporations can be complex and are sure to have many complex systems within. However, most of what is called *complex* is simply complicated. The causes and effects can be traced, and key players drive much of the results. Hence, traditional approaches to organization can be effective in improving performance.

The market is a different beast altogether. As a complex system, the market is hard to pin down with traditional, linear-based analysis. This complexity is one of the main reasons traditional economics or fundamental approaches (based on traditional finance assumptions) to investment meet with failure. Any successful approach to investing must start with a holistic view of the market.

EMERGENCE

One particular feature of CAS that deserves special mention is emergence. Holland's first experience with emergence came from his love of chess: "Chess was a game with just a small number of rules. And yet the incredible thing to us was that you never played the same game twice. The possibilities were just infinite."[33] Scientists generally defined emergence as "individual, localized behavior aggregat(ing) into global behavior that is…disconnected from its origins."[34] Hurricanes emerge from the positive feedback between wind, humidity, and the evaporation of warm water from the ocean.

Emergence in the market comes in the form of market patterns. No one is explicitly trying to create a trend or a range or volatility. It comes from within, as traders trade based on the price cues of other traders as well as the more explicit outlets of information. In concert and competition for the variety of their individual goals, traders create the market patterns and conditions that we see. These patterns and conditions are said to be *emergent properties* of the market.

The essence of emergence can be delineated in two ways. First, it is an endogenous phenomenon; and, second, it is unpredictable. Unpredictable in two ways: one, the result is unknown ahead of time; and two, it is independent of the agents that make up the CAS (i.e., the sum is not only greater than its parts, it has an existence all its own). In

---

33 Mitchell M. Waldrop, *Complexity: The Emerging Science at the Edge of Order and Chaos* (New York: Simon & Schuster Paperbacks, 1992).
34 John Miller and Scott Page, *Complex Adaptive Systems: An Introduction to Computational Models of Social Life* (New Jersey: Princeton University Press, 2007).

Holland and Miller's words, "(emergence) can be described without a detailed knowledge of the behavior of the individual agents."[35]

Agents follow the simple rules of behavior outlined by the CAS. For all its complexity, the market only allows two actions to its traders: buying and selling. Each trader buys and sells with his or her own goals in mind, and from these uncoordinated actions emerge all kinds of recognizable market patterns, such as trends, ranges, tops/bottoms, and support/resistance levels.

RANDOMNESS

Another key component to a CAS is randomness. Without randomness, connections would "harden"; the system would become static and eventually become extinct. Andrey Kolmogorov and Gregory Chaitin have done fascinating work in defining randomness in a useful way. They define randomness as extreme complexity; here, complexity refers to a very specific measure of *algorithmic information content*. The higher the content, the greater the complexity; the greater the complexity, the more random the system.

Think of an algorithm as a simple computer program. It is designed to follow a set of instructions to turn an input into an output. Because the set of instructions are an explicit to-do list, the program cannot speculate or guess as to what the user wants. Hence, the more order an object has, the easier it can be produced using an algorithm. Kolmogorov and Chaitin came up with an elegant measure of complexity: the size of the shortest algorithm that could produce a complete description of the object.

The shorter the algorithm, the lower the algorithmic information content and the greater the order; the longer the algorithm (i.e., the more complicated the set of instructions), the greater the algorithmic information content and the more randomness. For example, "sjsjsjsjsj" can easily be generated using a short algorithm—simply print "sj" five times. This string has low algorithmic information content. On the other hand, "sjlkgi8587198" has high algorithmic information content, because it is difficult to generate this output; one would have to create a long, unwieldy algorithm that replicates the input entirely (e.g., print "s," then print "j," then print "l," etc.). There is no order in this string, and the string cannot be *compressed* in any way, so that an algorithm can more easily generate it.

This string contains so much algorithmic information content that it can be judged random. Such disorder actually plays a very large role in our lives. Selecting people at random is considered fair play. Shuffling cards so they look more like the second example—that is, no recognizable patterns—prevents cheating. DNA contains a great deal of randomness, employing random mutations to provide novel sets of candidates to pop-

---

35 John H. Holland and John H. Miller, "Artificial Adaptive Agents in Economic Theory," *The American Economic Review* (1991).

ulate the next generation. This process of evolution has proven an effective method, so much so that a class of problem-solving technologies or search heuristics has been invented and become widely used.

Genetic algorithms (GA) are the most popular search heuristics. These will be discussed throughout the remainder of this book, with a GA-evolved trading system presented in the final section. By way of introduction, a GA is evolution boiled down to a formula. Part of that formula contains a random variable in order to introduce novel solutions as a way to improve the system. Without that variable, a CAS would simply recycle existing solutions, recombining until everything has been tried.

Edgar Peters, in his enlightening book, *Complexity, Risk, and Financial Markets*,[36] talks about the *necessity* of uncertainty. Through uncertainty a market is able to diversify its possible paths of development, thereby providing "opportunity for everyone, but the advantage to no one." In fact, "uncertainty is the market's main source of *stability* and *innovation*" (emphasis mine). Randomness and uncertainty will be discussed throughout the remainder of this book.

UNCOMFORTABLE THOUGHTS, PART I

Complexity theory is such a rich field; the previous section just sketched an outline of relevant aspects. But even with just a taste of the entirely new ways complexity theory looks at the world, the reader may already be feeling conceptual barriers rooted deep in his or her worldview. So, before proceeding further, it may be beneficial to address some of the anomalous concepts and paradigms complexity theory presents. Making a paradigm shift in these key areas may help adopt a more nuanced view of the market and investing in general.

There are four main dichotomies that illustrate key differences in a complexity world view:

1) linear vs. nonlinear
2) central command vs. decentralization
3) design vs. evolution
4) certainty vs. uncertainty

Linear vs. Nonlinear The majority of investors seem compelled to hone in on a single cause that will explain everything. The election made the stock market go up. Government spending will boost/tank equity indices. As of this writing, the back-and-forth partisan debate over raising the debt limit is the cause du jour of everything from treasuries to the S&P to the crude oil markets.

---

36 Edgar E. Peters, *Complexity, Risk, and Financial Markets* (Hoboken, NJ: Wiley, 2001).

There certainly does seem to be a bias toward simple images or concepts over complicated ones, reinforced constantly by the media (which, of course, is the main source of information for most investors). Themes, marketing hooks, sounds bites, and attention-grabbing headlines dominate information flows. It is easier and more comforting to discuss easy-to-understand concepts during meetings, especially as managers are constantly besieged by demands on their time and attention.

Much of this bias stems from taking a linear assumption of the market. People are accustomed to thinking that one cause will lead to one effect—that effect being something one can predict clearly and with certainty. But the market is nonlinear: market prices (output) do not correspond proportionally to its inputs (information or trader decisions). Nobody really knows what effect the new president will have on the S&P 500, if any at all. Good GDP reports can make the market go up, but cause it to fall if lower than expected.

Central Command vs. Decentralization People are also heavily accustomed to centralized command structures. Leaders and controllers in various forms are sought after where none exist, some *one* thing to teach, guide, and direct. Human intelligence and direction is needed to tame the wild forces of nature. After several modern-day cycles of government intervention exacerbating economic crises, people still cry out to politicians in times of distress, even as they are excoriated. Regulators are needed to prop up down markets. Reduced down to its essence, a stock market crash is simply the market adjusting to its environment, albeit in a way that is painful for many. As such, there is nothing wrong with the market, so that it needs to be regulated further.

However, governments, regulators, and large funds all cannot control the markets. That is not to say they cannot *influence* the market. But even this influence tends to be much smaller than one would think. In reality, the market is structured to find support and sustenance from a multitude of traders of all different sizes with widely disparate interests. In an effort to continue its function (providing liquidity), it *seeks out* traders with different interests, styles, and investment methods. As a result, (successful) markets will always be a faceless beast with no master.

Design vs. Evolution Another difficulty stems from the paradigm that order is *created not evolved*. Many intelligent and educated people still cling to the idea that anything with order and organization must be created, that it cannot evolve. After all, how can a computer just happen together? How can something as simple and mindless as evolution create something so complex as a computer? Surely a higher-order intelligence is needed to create something of this kind.

In *Darwin's Dangerous Idea,* Dennett elucidates the essence of the evolutionary process with a metaphor called the Library of Babel.[37] The Library of Babel is a thought experiment borrowed from Argentine poet Jorge Luis Borges's *Labyrinths* (1962). The Library is an imaginary storehouse of every *possible* book. Take all the letters of every

---

37 Daniel C. Dennett, *Darwin's Dangerous Idea* (New York: Simon & Schuster Paperbacks, 1995). For a much more articulate discussion of this topic, please see Eric Beinhocker's *Origin of Wealth,* p. 233.

alphabet, combined with spaces, numbers, and grammatical expressions, and consider every possible combination of a book. Most of the books obviously would not make sense; that is, many books would be replete with empty spaces, or 0s, or meaningless combinations of Greek letters.

However, some of these books would be quite interesting. Dennett points out that "one of (these books) is the best, most accurate 500-page biography of you, from the moment of your birth until the moment of your death." Unfortunately, because the Library contains all possible combinations of books, "locating (your biography)…would be all but impossible…since the Library also contains kazillions of volumes that are magnificently accurate biographies of you up till your tenth, twentieth, thirtieth, fortieth…birthday, and completely false about subsequent events of your life….But even finding one readable volume in this huge storehouse is unlikely in the extreme."[38]

Dennett goes on to describe what he calls the Library of Mendel, which would contain all possible genomes. Libraries such as these represent all the possible *designs* in the universe. Among the collections in this Library would be a computer. What evolution does is search through this space of possible designs and *find* the computer.

More specifically, evolution would, in search of something that would optimize deductive reasoning, find von Neumann's ideas, Turing's inventions, and a host of other simpler building blocks, and through its own special algorithm (competitive natural selection combined with reproduction and random mutation) it would evolve a computer. The computer itself, then, becomes a building block with which other solutions can be evolved.

The key point here is that things are not created from nothing, but rather *found*. Those that are found become building blocks for more complex products. In this way, order is evolved, not created. When the environment changes and presents new problems, existing solutions are scrapped for better ones. In the same way, the market, through the faceless, mindless process of evolution, evolves order, continuously cycling through its library of patterns and using those to create novel patterns in its unending quest to maximize liquidity.

Certainty vs. Uncertainty The previous section started a discussion on randomness that is continued here. Understanding why randomness is needed requires a detour through evolution. Daniel Dennett famously described evolution as an all-purpose algorithm used by all to create all.[39] The practical version of that algorithm is the genetic algorithm (GA). Rather than a problem-solving technique, a GA is a solution-finding technique. It does this by using the evolutionary process found in the DNA. Instead of genes, solutions are manipulated by a GA.

To find or evolve a solution to a problem, a GA will:

---

38 Ibid.
39 Ibid.

1) Create a starting population of possible solutions
2) Calculate which ones are the best, using some evaluation measure
3) Assign the best ones parental duty; these become the second generation (reproduction), with the bad solutions dropping out of the population (natural selection)
4) Combine the parents in two ways: sex and random mutations. The sex serves to spread whatever traits made the parents the best. Random mutations introduce novelty to diversify the population.
5) Go back to the second step

Notice that sex and random mutations are key components at the heart of the evolutionary process. Without random mutation, after a few generations people would all look the same, act the same, and think the same, as sex collects all the successful traits and spreads them throughout the population. Randomness is not a bad thing; along with sex, it's responsible for all the innovation, creativity, diversity, and freedom in this beautiful world.

A GA is a solution-seeking algorithm. Technically, it's referred to as a *search heuristic*, in that it's searching for a solution. Now think of all the possible solutions out there for a given problem. Give each solution a rating on how well it solves the problem. A good way to visualize this is to put all the solutions onto a three-dimensional graph. The Y-axis represents the rating, or "fitness value." Some solutions will be tall, as they are good solutions, but most will be on the ground, with zero fitness value. Some solutions will be scattered around, while a bunch of solutions will be clustered together. These solutions share common traits that give them high fitness values.

This topology is called a *search space,* and scientists use geographical terms to describe it. What a GA is designed to do is to scour this landscape, looking for those solutions with high fitness values. Once it finds one, it will scour the surrounding areas for a slightly different solution that might have a higher fitness value. Iterating this process over and over is called optimization, with the optimal solution the one in that cluster of solutions with the highest fitness value.

Now every generation weeds out bad solutions in order to get higher fitness values. The generation becomes more optimal as the solutions become more similar, with slight differences giving them the edge. Eventually the GA reaches the top of a hill—the hill being the cluster of solutions. And then it is stuck. Because the bad solutions were weeded out continuously, there are no more solutions to search. This optimal solution is called a *local maximum.*

Many local maxima exist on a given search space. The problem is, a search cannot tell in advance which hill it is climbing. It could start searching for a solution on a very low local maximum or, if lucky, a very high one. But the absolute best solution, the global maximum, is still out there, waiting to be found. It cannot get there, however, if it is stuck on a local maximum.

And this is where randomness comes into play. With a random mutation, the GA searches in a completely different area of the search space. In effect, it allows the search to jump around to different areas of the search space and frees it from the confines of a localized optimization. As a CAS, the market is also searching for solutions to survive and thrive. To get better, a market must adapt by continuously searching for new avenues of liquidity.

Anytime one source of influence on the market becomes too strong, it restricts liquidity. Good markets react by changing regimes (market modes and patterns), searching for other flows of funds. Edgar Peters is very articulate on this subject:

> The stock market exists to give investors a venue for trading. Investors want to make as much money as possible. However, the market, as an entity, does not have this goal. The market exists to provide liquidity, plain and simple. Therefore, it is in the market's interest to make itself as complex as possible. The end result is always the rise and fall of prices and the transfer of wealth....No *one* investment approach will work all of the time, at least in the short term. Many approaches will work *some* of the time. So, the market needs uncertainty if it is to offer opportunity to all investors. It also needs uncertainty to perpetuate the flow of funds between investors and to ensure its own survival. By ensuring that no specific information set drives the market every time, the market diversifies the nature of its own participants.[40]

Any experienced investor will have noticed this regime changing of the market. His or her strategy works great for a while and then stops. Then the investor notices that a different strategy works well, only to find, after switching, that it too stops after some time. Toby Crabel[41] once noted in an investment seminar that if one has a good trading system that worked for a while and is not currently working, one should not throw it away. That market condition is likely to come back and make the system profitable again. It is the adaptive nature of the market that causes this to occur.

EXAMPLE OF A CAS

CASs are all around us, but unless their paradigms are adopted to some degree, it is difficult to truly appreciate the dynamics of a CAS. One of the profound discoveries about a CAS is that all kinds of complex behavior can arise from very simple agents (the actors that make up the CAS, e.g., traders in a market, ants in an ant colony).

---

40 Edgar E. Peters, *Complexity, Risk, and Financial Markets* (Hoboken, NJ: Wiley, 2001).
41 Toby Crabel is a legend in the system trading industry who manages Crabel Capital Management (www.crabel.com).

Considered one of the simplest of creatures, ants are capable of cooperating to create a colony and perform a number of complex tasks. Perhaps the best work on complexity theory for the layman, *Complexity: A Guided Tour* by Melanie Mitchell provides a wonderful explanation of the ant colony as a CAS. Mitchell draws upon the work of ecologist Deborah Gordon, who identifies four main tasks of ants: foraging, nest-maintenance, patrolling, and refuse-sorting.[42]

An ant will change its role and change tasks, according to environmental changes. For example, if the nest is intruded upon, the number of nest maintenance workers will increase. If the food supply increases, ants will switch to foraging tasks.

How does an ant know to switch jobs without a central controller looking over the entire colony and forest floor and command it to? Ants switch jobs based on what the environment does and what other ants do. Specifically, ants are stimulated to switch tasks based upon the rate at which they see other ants doing that task. In other words, if an inactive ant sees food, it is more likely to switch to forage mode. But it is also likely to switch to forage mode if it sees other ants doing the same thing.

So how are ants processing information? Mitchell is insightful here: "[I]nformation is not, as in a traditional computer, precisely or statically located in any particular place in the system. Instead, it takes the form of statistics and dynamics of patterns over the system's components."[43]

No, ants do not have advanced degrees in statistics. What this means is that ants are using a form of sampling. Ants sample the number of ants doing nest maintenance work and are signaled to join in as well. "Eventually, the ants will have established a detailed map of paths to food sources. An observer might think that the ants are using a map supplied by an intelligent designer of food distribution. However, what appears to be a carefully laid out mapping of pathways to food supplies is really just a consequence of a series of random searches."[44]

The reason ant colonies and other CASs can thrive is because this type of decentralized system has many advantages. A CAS is robust because it does not depend on one commander, who, if killed off, would leave the colony vulnerable. The decentralized structure effectively turns every ant into a commander that can provide immediate feedback to the rest of the colony. This structure allows the colony to receive feedback quickly and, hence, adapt faster.

Mitchell cites another advantage of the CAS structure of the ant colony, which Douglas Hofstadter called a "parallel terraced scan." Many different areas are scanned simultaneously or in parallel, but they are terraced in that some possibilities are scanned more quickly and carefully. Because ants can communicate with each other, the scanning is continuously adjusted to more efficiently find a solution.

---

42 Melanie Mitchell, *Complexity: A Guided Tour* (New York: Oxford University Press, 2008).
43 Ibid.
44 Ibid.

Similarly, ant foraging uses a parallel-terraced-scan strategy: many ants initially explore random directions for food. If food is discovered in an one these directions, more of the system's resources (ants) are allocated, via the feedback mechanisms described above, to explore those directions further. At all times, different paths are dynamically allocated exploration resources in proportion to their relative promise... However, due to the large number of ants and their intrinsic random elements, unpromising paths continue to be explored as well, though with many fewer resources. After all, who knows-a better source of food might be discovered.[45]

This model of searching and scanning shares many similarities with a GA. In fact, ant colony optimization algorithms are another class of search heuristics that scientists use to solve problems.

MODELS OF MARKET BEHAVIOR

In the markets, traders communicate with each other in a similar way, by sampling and copying the actions of other traders around them. This type of sampling behavior has a more common name: herding. Herding has been identified as a common behavior in markets, responsible for creating trends. Most famously, Robert Prechter, of Elliott Wave International, has written extensively on the topic and created a think tank called The Socionomic Foundation to research this phenomenon.

Described as "History's Hidden Engine," socionomics posits that large trends in society and the market are driven by social *mood*. If the society at large is *feeling* positive, constructive behavior ensues, such as cooperation between governments, a rising stock market, expanding economy, box-shaped cars, and brighter fashion tones. A negative mood will cause society to go to war, the stock market to decline, a recession/depression, rounder-shaped cars, and darker fashion tones.

Socionomics is counterintuitive in that most people believe events *cause* social mood. The stock market goes up, and investors feel happy. Socionomics believes that a society that feels happy, for whatever prior cause, will buy stocks. It is the mood that causes the event. This mood is generated and reinforced through the herding mechanism.[46]

Herding behavior is simply acting the way others do. It is a type of sampling heuristic and, like cognitive biases, is triggered in times of uncertainty. When uncertain about what to do, most will default to following the actions of others. The socionomic model of herding describes it as "a model of *unconscious*, *prerational* herding behavior that posits *endogenous* dynamics that have *evolved* in *homogenous* groups of humans in

---

45 Ibid.
46 Prechter (1979, 1999, 2001, 2003). See also www.socionomics.net.

contexts of *uncertainty*, while eschewing the traditional economic assumptions of *equilibrium* and *utility-maximization*."[47]

Herding behavior manifests itself dramatically in the form of trends. Markets are no different, and herding causes both bull and bear markets. Acute herding creates the wave three in a trend. In Elliott wave analysis, wave threes are the strongest, most sustainable part of a trend. This is when the majority of participants are betting in the same direction. Most of these participants are herding; self-reinforcement causes more and more bets in the same direction.

A critical component of the socionomic model is that herding is entirely endogenous, that is, the outcome's causes are internal to the system. There is no single cause that starts the trend; in this way, herding exhibits complex properties. Robert J. Shiller's *Investor Behavior in the October 1987 Stock Market Crash: Survey Evidence* found that although investors calmly reasoned (during the crash) that the cause of the crash was that the market was overvalued, their concurrent actions at the time of the crash were completely the opposite of calm and reasonable. Shiller found these institutional investors to be "…people reacting to each other with heightened attention and emotion, trying to fathom what other investors were likely to do, and falling back on intuitive models.…" Shiller's research further found that there was little in the way of relevant news, rumors, or events during the crash and that there was "…no recognizable exogenous trigger for the crash."

An alternative model is what Walker and Prechter refer to as the *medical model theory* of herding.[48] These models focus on contagion, or the wild, rapid spread of diseases. Here the "disease" is panic, and the best-known work is by Morgan Kelly and Cormac O'Grada, two professors at the University College Dublin School of Economics.

In "Market Contagion: Evidence from the Panics of 1854 and 1857,"[49] the researchers take an interesting approach to modeling complex behavior by examining the social networks of then-recent Irish immigrants living in New York and these networks' role in two separate market panics. They study two financial panics during the 1850s that resulted in bank runs. Bank runs generally are characterized as fear-induced panic attacks, where depositors close their accounts and pull their funds out en masse simultaneously.

They studied the records of bank accounts held at the Emigrant Industrial Savings Bank (EISB) in New York. The majority of the account holders were recent immigrants from Ireland. After studying the individual characteristics of the depositors and their account histories, they looked for the main characteristics of depositors who closed ac-

47 Wayne D. Parker and Robert R. Prechter, "Herding: An Interdisciplinary Integrative Review from a Socionomic Perspective" (International Conference on Cognitive Economics, Sofia, Bulgaria, 2005).
48 Ibid.
49 Cormac O'Grada and Morgan Kelly, " Market Contagion: Evidence from the Panics of 1854 and 1857," *American Economic Review* (2000): 90.

counts and left the bank (panickers) in comparison to those who kept their accounts and stayed with the bank (stayers).

So what was the number one characteristic that distinguished panickers from stayers? County of origin in Ireland. "Depositors from one set of counties tended to close their accounts in both panics, while otherwise identical individuals from other counties tended to stay with the bank." Further, "county of origin also determines, in the more important run, the timing of panicking: different groups of depositors closed their accounts at different times" (footnote).

By comparing marriage records, they ascertained that Irish couples who married during in New York during the 1850s did indeed come from the same Irish county. These couples and others like them wound up living in the same buildings. "Consequently, if a depositor had emigrated from County Cork in Ireland, we can be quite confident that he knew other depositors from Cork."[50]

The tendency for immigrants to cluster is strong. In 1855 New York, while Irish immigrants made up 28 percent of the city's population, they made up 40 percent of the First, Fourth, and Sixth Wards. Further, Irish immigrants from particular regions of Ireland clustered together: "Monroe Street was known as 'Cork Row,' in the Fourth Ward the area next to the East River was 'favorable spot for Kerry men and their descendants.'"

The key mechanism that spreads the contagion is a social network. Here, researchers analyzed marriage patterns based on records from a church located near the EISB. Nearly 70 percent of the marriages during 1853–1860 were from couples who had lived in the same or neighboring counties. Examining the addresses of the depositors also showed that numerous people with different last names had the same addresses.

The researchers then examined the activity of the depositors during the two panics. This data was then organized by county origin and home address. After adjusting for statistical effects, they found clear patterns of contagion behavior with depositors from the same address or from the same county acting the same way (i.e., either panicking or staying). "In 1857, for example, while 52% of accounts in our sample closed during the panic, only 17% of depositors originally from Donegal and 26% from Cavan (both Ulster counties) panicked, compared with 67% for Meath and 75% from Kerry." Further, it was found that the same behavior occurred during both panics.

Another interesting model of herding behavior was found in ant foraging. Alan Kirman was vocal about the failures of traditional economics in the aftermath of the subprime crisis. His work on agent-based modeling contributes further to the complexity view of the markets. Briefly, agent-based modeling studies the interactions of autonomous agents and the global phenomena that emerge. As autonomous agents go, ants seem to be an ideal example.

Kirman starts his account by citing the results of an experiment by Deneuboug et al. (1987a) and Pasteels et al. (1987), where two identical food sources were offered to ants. They were replenished so that they remained identical. Ants, after a period of time, were

---

50 Ibid.

found not to be split 50/50 as common sense would conclude, but rather 80/20. Kirman further noted that this 80/20 split would often reverse inexplicably.[51] This phenomenon is mirrored in studies by Becker where only one of two similar restaurants on opposite sides of the street tended to attract long lines of customers.

Although characterized a bit differently, Kirman's account confirms Mitchell's in that ants stimulate one another to mimic their behavior, in order to rapidly maximize the acquisition of possible food sources. Kirman draws upon his studies of herding behavior and applies them to market behavior. Robert Shiller and John Pound have also done significant work in this area. They point out that "interpersonal communication among peers seems to produce the kind of attention and reassurance that leads to changes in behavior" and concluded in their paper that investors in stocks whose price had increased dramatically were "less likely to be systematic, were more influenced by interpersonal communications, talked more to others, were more enthusiastic and optimistic."[52]

BEHAVIORAL FINANCE MODELS OF MARKET BEHAVIOR

Cognitive biases and prospect theory are great advances in psychology that help make sense of investing in real time. Taking a step further, more recent work in behavioral finances does much to explain how these forces manifest themselves in market patterns. From the outset, it should be noted that there are numerous patterns that emerge in the markets. Much of time, there are no patterns whatsoever, as the market meanders randomly. Efficient Market Hypothesis's main problem is in trying to explain all market behavior as efficient. But no one regime ever dominates the market for too long; a market does exhibit efficient behavior from time to time, as do trending, ranging, mean-reverting, noisy behaviors.

Some of the most interesting work in behavioral finance has been authored by Richard Thaler, currently the Ralph and Dorothy Keller Distinguished Service Professor of Behavioral Science and Economics at The University of Chicago Booth School of Business. In his book, *The Winner's Curse*, he presents the case for mean-reverting behavior in the market as based on cognitive biases exhibited by investors.

Thaler cites a couple of long-term studies that reveal mean reversion in US stocks. French and Roll (1986) repeated Fama's 1965 study of serial correlation (market price series are correlated to themselves and, hence, predictable) by extending the time period for more data and found significant mean reversion. A longer-term study by Fama and French revealed even greater mean reversion.

---

51 Alan Kirman, "Ants, Rationality, and Recruitment," *The Quarterly Journal of Economics*, 108 (1993).

52 Robert J. Shiller and John Pound, "Survey Evidence on Diffusion of Interest among Institutional Investors," *Journal of Economics Behavior and Organization* (1986).

If mean reversion exits, then countertrend strategies should work. In fact, Thaler cites research by Basu (1977), Keim (1985), Rosendberg, and Reid and Lanstein (1985) that shows such strategies can indeed generate positive, excess returns. In a 1985 paper, Thaler, along with DeBondt, researched this topic as well in the hopes of finding a link between countertrend strategies and "systematic investor overreaction."[53]

Specifically, Recency Bias (ReB) was identified as the cognitive bias that leads to this overreaction, although the 1987 paper did not express it explicitly. Thaler studied monthly data of all NYSE stocks from 1926–1982. He identified a group of extreme winners over a five-year period and a group of extreme losers over the same period. Each group was then followed for the next five years. What was found was that the extreme winners underperformed the market average over the next five years, and the extreme losers outperformed the market average over the next five years. Had an investor executed a mean-reversion strategy on these stocks during this period, he or she would have made between 5 and 8 percent returns. In a subsequent paper, Thaler and DeBondt explained overreaction in market price movement as stemming from "people's intuitive forecasts (having) a tendency to overweight salient information such as recent news, and underweight less salient data such as long-term averages."[54]

UNDER- AND OVERREACTION

More detailed research into overreaction was conducted by numerous researchers, finding evidence of cognitive biases leading to under- and overreaction in the markets. Many common cognitive biases come into play, leading to irrational behavior. One well-known model is that proposed by Daniel, Hirshleifer, and Subrahmanyan (1998), referred to as DHS. The DHS model has been verified by Kausar and Taffler in their paper, "Testing Behavioral Finance Models of Market Under- and Overreaction: Do They Really Work?" (2005). DHS build their model on cognitive biases surrounding private research; private research is the investor's interpreted research from publically available information.

As investors come up with their own conclusions, they exhibit overconfidence bias, thereby overevaluating the accuracy of their conclusions. They then make investment decisions based on their research, either buying or selling, and then continue buying or overbuying, reinforced by the endowment bias. This overbuying leads to price extensions, momentum, or trend continuation. From here, if the market continues in the direction of the initial investment, the investor will exhibit ever greater overconfidence due to two other biases: confirmation bias and self-attribution bias (see chapter 2).

Confirmation bias causes investors to add to their existing positions in response to news that confirm their original decisions. If they hear bad news that contradicts their original

---

53 Richard Thaler, *The Winner's Circle* (Princeton: Princeton University Press, 1992).
54 Werner F. M. DeBondt and Richard Thaler, "Do Security Analysts Overreact?" *American Economic Review* (1990).

decision, the self-attribution bias will "shield" this private research from criticism or the necessary corrections. Losses resulting from private research will be attributed to bad luck rather than a deficiency in the private research. Thus, repeated cycles of investing under the self-attribution bias will actually strengthen the confidence of investors' private research, whether they hear good or bad news.

COMPLEXITY MODELS OF MARKET BEHAVIOR

It is tempting to think that, when ranges start to expand and a trend forms after a long congestion period, some large buyer has entered the market. The media is always identifying such culprits with catchy headlines (e.g., "Failure of Debt Deal Prompts Big Sell-Off"). Adam Ponzi and Y. Aizawa's paper, "Evolutionary Financial Market Models,"[55] demonstrates that such trends occur purely from the interactions of traders.

The researchers were motivated by an analogous phenomenon called *punctuated equilibrium*. This view in the field of evolution states that evolutionary change does not happen gradually, as commonly thought, but that it happens all of a sudden, rapidly, after periods where nothing happens. Stephen Jay Gould and Niles Eldredge, in their landmark classic, state:

> We believe that punctuational change dominates the history of life; evolution is concentrated in very rapid events of speciation...(the gradual evolutionary view) was an a priori assertion from the start—it was never "seen" in the rocks; it expressed the cultural and political biases of 19th century liberalism....We think that it has now become an empirical fallacy.[56]

Further, the researchers extend the theory to sudden "avalanches" of extinctions (think dinosaurs) that also happen abruptly, after periods of peace and calm or stasis.

In the Ponzi/Aizawa model, traders are connected via a neural net. The connection vector determines how trader *i* will be influenced by trader *j*. The connection strength, or weight, between traders determines the *degree* to which each *listens to* or is influenced by the other to his or her position, bull or bear (i.e., the probability that *i* will change his or her position to *j*'s position). These connections can be positive or negative; a positive connection causes one trader to listen to the other, whereas a negative connection will lower the influence.

Traders hold on to positions as they listen to their "friends"—traders who hold the same position—and stop listening to their "enemies"—traders who hold opposite posi-

---

55 Adam Ponzi and Y. Aizawa, "Evolutionary Financial Market Models," *Physica* (2000).
56 Stephen Jay Gould and Niles Eldredge, "Punctuated Equilibria: The Tempo and Mode of Evolution Reconsidered," *Paleobiology* (1977).

tions. Traders are grouped into two different "types": confident and unsure. The confident traders will hold on to their positions, while the unsure traders will constantly flip their positions.

Further, the varying degrees of influence between traders is modified with the use of an evolutionary algorithm; this algorithm allows the traders to vary their levels of influence. The model finds that under these conditions, *unsure traders will generally gravitate toward the position of the confident traders*. Their positions can be either bull or bear. This mimics the herding phenomenon seen in real markets.

During this period, the market price created by the trader's interactions with each other is marked with low volatility. However, once the unsure traders take the same position as the confident traders, thus creating a majority of confident traders on one side of the market, volatility explodes. This volatility explosion looks very similar to the ones seen in real markets. There are no exogenous shocks, no "big hands," no government default—none of these are required to replicate the kind of volatility explosions seen in the markets. They occur through the complex interaction of dynamically linked agents.

ECONOPHYSICS

The term *econophysics* was coined by H. Eugene Stanley to describe the host of papers written by physicists to explain economic and financial phenomena. Econophysicists most frequently utilize concepts and models taken from statistical physics, such as stochastic processes (random, dispersion models) and nonlinear dynamics (chaos, criticality, power laws). Most pertinent to complexity theory is the area of self-organized criticality.

Self-organized criticality is a field of physics that studies dramatic events that occur spontaneously. Earthquakes, volcanic eruptions, turbulence, and political upheaval seem to occur of their own accord, with specific mechanisms that push the system into such volatile states. Miller and Page describe critical events as a specific instance of a general class of emergent patterns in CASs. Self-organized criticality is described mathematically by a power law.

Power law distributions are commonly seen in the activities of complex systems. A power law underlies the commonly known 80/20 rule, the Paretian curve/distribution, and heavy/fat/long-tail distributions. Two variables have a power law relationship when the frequency of x occurring is equal to the size of x raised to the $-y$th power. In other words, the smaller x is, the more likely it is to occur; also, the greater it is, the less likely it is to occur. Thus, systems that are driven by power laws have many small events and a few big ones.

The number of long-tail phenomena and other manifestations of power laws is surprisingly large. Earthquakes and volcanic eruptions are commonly cited examples. The distribution of income in societies, sizes of cities, forest fires, words in most languages, family names, popularity of books and music, and movie sales are more common examples.

The big knock on traditional economics is that long-tail phenomena (e.g., bubbles, crises, trends) should not happen, because market prices are modeled after the Gaussian function where prices are pulled toward the mean, resulting in the bell curve. In a bell curve, large events are too rare to be of concern. However, bubbles and crises do occur— and *more often than a bell curve would suggest.* In fact, econophysicists would argue that prices in a market are not *normally* distributed; rather, they are leptokurtic, where large events are rare but more common than traditional economists would like to believe.

In reality, the markets are full of fat-tail events, from large trends to tight ranges. These patterns occur far more often and last far longer than traditional economists predict. Watch the mini-S&P for the entirety of the twenty-three hours it trades on a one-minute time frame. One will see a large number of small bars and a few very large bars. However, the frequency of these sizes occur on a regular basis. Trading these types of patterns is how the bulk of trading profits are made.

Self-organized criticality has become a popular model for explaining how a market can form bubbles and crashes without any external influence. Developed by Per Bak, criticality theory states that individual agents interacting with each lead them to organize and converge to critical points. Bak first coined the term after work in phase transitions led him to ask the more general question of how order arises from disorder.

Before reaching that state, any one agent acting on another has only localized effects, that is, it only affects those agents directly in contact with each other. Upon reaching a critical state, however, actions by a small number of agents can affect globalized behavior, where power law behavior is seen. That is, the entire system, once critical, becomes "very sensitive" to even the smallest of disturbances and can lead the entire system into catastrophic behavior.

Bak's original experiment was with sand piles. Adding a grain of sand to a sand pile in the initial stages does little to the entire pile. But continue adding, and the pile eventually reaches its angle of repose, waiting to fall into an avalanche. At this critical point, adding single grains of sand will start small avalanches that can accumulate into one massive avalanche. The magnitude of this avalanche exhibits a power law relationship to its frequency.

In a paper co-authored by Kan Chen, Jose Scheinkman, and M. Woodford while at the Santa Fe Institute, titled "Self Organized Criticality and Fluctuations in Economics,"[57] Bak builds a toy model of a large, dynamically connected economy and finds endogenously created order after evolving into a critical state. After using a dissipative dynamical system (open systems where energy is drawn in and then eventually dissipated) to explain the regular occurrence of fat-tail events in earthquakes and biological phenomena, Bak applies this approach to economics. Similar to traders in a market, economic sectors

---

57 Per Bak, Ken Chan, Jose Scheinkman, and M. Woodford, "Self Organized Criticality and Fluctuations in Economics" (Santa Fe: Santa Fe Institute, 1992).

(agents) interact with each other by buying and selling to each other, according to each other's supply and demand needs.

The model starts with random orders for goods. If the supplier has the quantity in stock, it sells it; if not, it produces two units, one to fill the order and one to put in inventory. The supplier itself must order from its suppliers. Thus, a chain reaction of ordering/production is created. When all orders are filled, the chain reaction stops.

What the researchers are looking for are avalanches of ordering/production that stem from the initial first purchase order, or what they call a shock (the system of suppliers is inactive until one single order from the initial supplier "shocks" the system into production mode). In one sample simulation run, one order resulted in eight layers of suppliers ordering from each other to fill that order.

So what would happen if there were multiple independent orders? Avalanches of production. A large number of productions stops shortly, whereas a few extend significantly—the size of which, compared to the others, are fat-tailed. Analyzing the results, Bak and his colleagues found that this model does indeed organize itself into a critical point where avalanches occur regularly.

In this model, it is the relationship between suppliers that affects the avalanches. If suppliers could somehow produce without ordering from other suppliers, nothing of the sort would happen. These supplier relationships put them in the same kind of influence network of traders demonstrated in the models above.

THE SANTA FE ARTIFICIAL STOCK MARKET

This chapter concludes with a market model based on complexity theory in its most "orthodox" form. Brian Arthur, John Holland, and colleagues at the Santa Fe Institute were able to model a unique stock market, using the core components of complexity theory.[58] It is an example of an agent-based model in that it is built from the ground up, with no underlying assumptions about the market or trading.

The model is then able to examine what would happen if traders were allowed to evolve on their own. What would the market look like? What emergent properties might the market generate? Specifically, the researchers were interested in whether the market would settle on an equilibrium under the rational expectations model (traditional economics) or behave more like a real market with bubbles, crashes, and high volatility.

Perhaps the most interesting feature of the Santa Fe Institute model is the addition of a learning component to trading activities. Using a GA to allow traders to evolve trading strategies, the model mimics real-life traders learning from their mistakes, copying successful strategies used by other traders, and discarding strategies that do not work.

---

58 Brian Arthur, J. H. Holland, B. LeBaron, R. Palmer, and P. Tayler, "Asset Pricing Under Endogenous Expectations in an Artificial Stock Market," SFI Paper 96-12-093, *Economic Notes* (1997).

With the objective of maximizing profits, the agents in the model not only trade with each other to create market prices, but also co-evolve.

GAs will be discussed in greater detail in the final chapter. Briefly, a GA is a formula that mimics natural evolution. Holland is largely credited with popularizing the GA as a way to observe complex emergent behavior, describe the underlying process of evolution, and expound its use as a general search heuristic. Here, the GA is a convenient way to account for learning behavior in traders. Part of the GA introduces novel strategies into the model via random mutation. By adjusting a randomly chosen part of a successful strategies, new variants (thinks mutants) are tried and traded by the agents.

Through this process of reproducing successful strategies (reproduction), generating new variants of those strategies (random mutation), and testing their efficacy in the market (natural selection), traders continually adapt to changing markets, while their interactions continuously create market behavior. Because no other data are provided from outside the model, traders use the market prices they themselves have created to inform their activities: "agents have to form their expectations from their anticipations of other agents' expectations, and this self-reference precludes expectations being formed by deductive means." Thus, this model is wholly endogenous.

Specifically, the model creates individual agents represented by simple algorithms, that is, they have the ability to collect and process information (input), make decisions (output), and receive feedback (evolution). These trading agents are "artificially" intelligent in that they are given GA capabilities to evolve their own strategies.

A simulated stock market was created with a single stock that paid a random dividend. The market price would be determined by the buying and selling of trading agents. The goal for each agent was predictive accuracy. The input, or information each agent based his or her decisions on, were threefold: historical prices, historical dividend payout, and a risk-free interest rate (i.e., they could stay out of the stock market and stay in cash). Each agent had a population of one hundred strategies initially; these form the initial population of strategies with which the GA could evolve successive generations of strategies. Each trading agent had a choice of investing in the stock or receiving a fixed interest rate in a bank account (staying in cash).

What they found was surprising. When the GA parameters are set at a low rate, such that the trading agents adapt slowly, the market finds an equilibrium as predicted by EMH. When the parameters are set high, such that traders adapt at a more realistic rate, "the market self-organizes into a complex pattern. It acquires a rich psychology, technical trading emerges, temporary bubbles and crashes occur, and asset prices and trading volume show statistical features [e.g. volatility clustering]…characteristic of actual market data."[59] Most notable was the evolution of technical trading strategies by the trading agents without any prior knowledge of technical analysis. The researchers note that these technical trading strategies worked, in spite of traditional economists' prediction that such strategies cannot generate alpha.

---

59   Ibid.

Sound familiar? Traders evolving and interacting with other traders create all kinds of complex market patterns that have nothing to do with changes in the underlying economic value of the stock. In other words, all the order and chaos of the markets was created with simple trading agents acting according to the specified rules of a CAS. Further, no one agent had any advantage from the beginning (e.g., more money, insider information). There was no central controller directing price movement. Without either of these, the market was able to organize itself into trends and ranges. There was no major event, no collusion, no "big hands," no government intervention that caused big moves in the market. Also interesting was that bubbles and crashes were seen as well, without any of the usual suspects of late. If the big money is made on such moves, one need look no further than the market itself.

Another notable feature of the model is that EMH behavior was found if the model assumed that traders did not learn or adapt to each other and the market. The switch occurs, depending on how slowly or quickly trading agents adapt. What constitutes slow and fast? Slow adaptation does not allow for a realistic rate of learning new strategies based on current market conditions. The GA allows traders to observe and copy strategies that work and discard ones that do not work. It also allows traders to randomly mutate existing strategies to form new ones. The slow-learning group does not do this fast enough to find novel strategies that do better than existing ones. The market settles in an equilibrium proving traditional economists right, that is, it *proves that their assumptions about market participants are oversimplified*. In the previous sections on ant colonies, it was shown that ants are capable of evolving and adapting successfully. Traditional economists seem to think traders have a harder time learning than ant colonies.

The fast-learning group was able to successfully propagate novel strategies into the system. These new strategies were introduced fast enough to be adopted by other agents. Once reinforced thus, the market is taken into new price ranges via trends in an orderly fashion. Then, due to the competitive force of a CAS, the market will strike out into new areas, thus creating wholly different market patterns. Support and resistance levels were employed by traders in the experiments as well as momentum-based trading strategies.

Part of the evolutionary process (perhaps the most unnerving aspect) is that random events can become fixtures in a species. Arthur's famous examples of the creation of Silicon Valley and the adoption of VHS over beta formats show that the origins of such adoption are wholly random (i.e. the smaller beta format is actual more beneficial). But through a few, key random choices, VHS was able to take a foothold, after which positive feedback loops were created to establish its dominance (more manufacturers make it causing video stores to stock them, which causes manufacturers to create more VHS players, etc.). In a similar manner, the researchers speculate that this type of evolutionary pattern is responsible for the adoption of technical trading strategies:

Thus, technical analysis can emerge if trend following (or mean reversion) beliefs are by chance generated in the population, and if random perturbations in the dividend sequence activate and subsequently validate them. From then on, they may take their place in the population of patterns recognized by the agents and become mutually sustainable. This emergence of structure from the mutual interaction of system subcomponents justifies our using the label "complex" for this regime.[60]

CONCLUSION

The complex nature of the market presents a paradigm vastly different from that of traditional economics. The market is not primarily a price discovery mechanism, and it does not seek equilibrium, both of which would be consequences or results of a linear process. Perhaps the best way to characterize the difference in views is that complexity theory defines the market's goal or function as a *state* rather than as a *result*.

A complex system always has a function or purpose. This function is a state, not a result. The global ecosystem promotes the stable transfer of energy to maintain organic life. A free market economy promotes the trade of goods and services among participants who seek to increase their wealth. The goal of a complex system is not a static "equilibrium" but rather a dynamic, evolving state that is ever changing, ever creative, but ever stable.[61]

While many points in the complexity paradigm are incommensurable with that of traditional economics, complexity theory also exposes much of the flaws with traditional economics, especially in relation to investing. Seen from a complexity point of view, the markets do not lend themselves to the oversimplified, linear process inherent in most forms of fundamental discretionary investment. In the next chapter, these weaknesses will be exposed in full detail.

---

60 Ibid.

61 Edgar E. Peters, *Complexity, Risk, and Financial Markets* (Hoboken, NJ: Wiley, 2001).

CHAPTER 5. WHY FUNDAMENTAL INVESTING IS NOT RATIONAL

DISCRETIONARY INVESTING

Discretionary investing, as opposed to mechanical trading, makes investment decisions without a prescribed set of rules. When to enter and exit the market, which markets to trade, how much to trade, how much to risk—these decisions are made on the fly while the markets are in play. Some guidelines or a collection of trading rules may be employed, but when and how to use these is at the discretion of the investor.

Rather than placing the onus of decision making on a systematic set of explicit rules, discretionary investing depends entirely on the investor on a trade-by-trade basis. Proponents of this approach extol its flexibility. In truth, discretionary investing is simply the default approach adopted by the majority of investors, just because they are unaware of the alternatives.

Where the rubber meets the road is in the discrepancy between intended and actual action. If an investment opportunity is presented and not taken, this is a judgmental error. If a position is to be liquidated but is held onto a bit longer, this is also an error. To be able to evaluate one's investment success, such evaluations must be possible. However, without clearly specified rules, it is impossible to judge the efficacy of one's investment decisions.

Hence, with a lack of clear rules and procedures, investing often becomes a vague, inconsistent approach with ad hoc decisions made to no long-term effect. Prechter describes the futility of this approach:

> When I first began trading, I did what many others who start out in the markets do: I developed a list of trading rules. The list was created piecemeal, with each new rule garnered from books on trading. I would typically add one following the conclusion of an unsuccessful trade....The resulting list of do's and don'ts ultimately comprised 16 statements. About six months after the completion of my carved-in-stone list of trading rules, I balled up the paper and threw it in the trash... I realized that I made not merely a mistake here and there in the list, but a fundamental error in compiling the list in the first place. The error was in taking aim at the *last* trade....[62]

Practically, discretionary investing's numerous pitfalls open investors up to a host of problems that often go unseen. Chapters 2 and 3 covered many of the irrational tendencies of investors. Behavioral finance has demonstrated that, contrary to the general con-

---

62 Robert Prechter, *Prechter's Perspective* (Atlanta: New Classics Library, 1996).

sensus (especially that of traditional economists), the markets are not a place governed by reason, logic, and order. Investors do not act in such a way as to maximize profits. When probability and logic indicate the most profitable course of action is to buy, investors often sell. When it is best to stay out of the market, they dive in. When they should buy aggressively, they hesitate.

Note, these errors are for lack of knowledge or experience. Cognitive biases are *systemic* errors of judgment deeply rooted into human psychology. Centuries of evolution have created numerous heuristics that help man survive and thrive in simple situations. Heuristics that can handle uncertain and complex situations have yet to be evolved.

But it gets worse. It turns out intuitive reasoning, in general, has some serious flaws. Inherent structural problems with intuitive reasoning render it useless and harmful in complex situations. Extensional thinking, actuarial or statistical reasoning, is the only option available to make sound, rational decisions in the face of uncertainty and risk.

Considerable research stretching as far back as the 1950s shows that statistical reasoning is superior to intuitive reasoning. In a wide range of fields, trusting one's gut leads to significant mistakes, with negative consequences. Discretionary investors, without the use of an explicit decision framework (e.g., model, method, system) are, for the most part, relying on their intuition.

STATISTICAL VS. INTUITIVE REASONING

If intuitive reasoning is the basis of discretionary investing, statistical reasoning forms the basis for system trading. In the scientific literature, the discretionary form of predictive judgment is called clinical prediction or expert judgment, while statistical reasoning is referred to as actuarial prediction. A general class of "mechanical prediction" has been identified, which encompasses statistical, actuarial and algorithmic processes. Grove et al. provide a useful description of the two approaches to judgment:

> *Clinical judgment* refers to the typical procedure long used by applied psychologists and physicians, in which the judge puts data together using informal, subjective methods. Clinicians differ in how they do this: The very nature of the process tends to preclude precise specification. *Mechanical prediction,* including statistical prediction (using explicit equations), actuarial prediction (as with insurance companies' actuarial tables), and what we may call algorithmic prediction (e.g., a computer program emulating expert judges), is by contrast well specified. Once developed, application of mechanical prediction requires no expert judgment. Also, mechanical predictions are 100% reproducible.[63]

---

63 W. M. Grove, D. H. Zald, A. M. Hallberg, B. Lebow, E. Snitz, and C. Nelson, "Clinical versus mechanical prediction: A meta-analysis," *Psychological Assessment* (2000).

A significant amount of research has proven the superiority of the mechanical approach over clinical judgment in prediction. Most mechanical approaches begin with a statistical model. Hardman traces the origins of this approach to social judgment theory (SJT). "By applying statistical analysis to a series of such judgments it is possible to describe the impact that different cues (signals, indicators) have on a particular type of judgment. Additionally, SJT is concerned with the creation of statistical models...that can be used to predict future cases."[64]

A mathematical formula or algorithm is constructed and developed by testing on historical data. This algorithm becomes a model used to make predictions on new data. There are a great many tools that statistics provides with which to develop such models. Among the more common methods is multiple linear regression analysis (MLR), on which many artificial intelligence technologies are based (e.g., neural nets). MLR analysis allows for the different weights to be assigned to the salient indicators of the phenomenon that is to be predicted.

A trader might ask what the factors involved in predicting a trend might be. After identifying a variety of quantifiable indicators (e.g., trading volume, accelerating momentum), MLR can be used to tie in all these factors into one formula and assign weights to ascertain the importance of each indicator. Testing or training a model on past data might reveal that volume is a very significant indicator of trend and, hence, assign a 45 percent weight, whereas accelerating momentum is not important and assign a 15 percent weight. If an indicator is not a factor at all, it would be assigned 0 percent, whereas if only one indicator was necessary, it would be assigned 100 percent.

Many effective statistical models use simple linear regression, rather than MLR. Simple linear regression involves creating one simple formula to calculate one output number. Usually, that number is then used as a threshold to signal a decision. Hardman gives an example of a famous study conducted by Lewis Goldberg,[65] in which Goldberg was able to derive a simple formula based on scores from the Minnesota Multiphasic Personality Inventory (MMPI) that could distinguish between psychosis and neurosis. The rule manipulated MMPI scores to calculate a final score. If above the threshold figure of 45, the patient was diagnosed with psychosis; if below 45, the patient was neurotic.

Referred to now as the Goldberg Rule, this formula was tested against thirteen professional clinical psychologists in diagnosing patients. Out of 861 cases (out-of-sample), the Goldberg Rule correctly predicted 70 percent of the discharge diagnoses. The professionals' accuracy levels ranged from 50 to 67 percent. A simple statistical model had beaten the intuitive judgments of professional psychologists. These were Ph.D. professionals who had extensive experience with the MMPI.

---

64 David Hardman, *Judgment and Decision Making—Psychological Perspectives* (London: British Psychological Society and Blackwell Publishing, Ltd., 2009).

65 L. R. Goldberg, "Diganosticians vs. Diagnostic Signs," *Psychological Monographs* (1965).

The MMPI was developed with the help of Paul Meehl, the leading researcher in this field. His *Clinical Versus Statistical Prediction: A Theoretical Analysis and a Review of the Evidence* (1954) is the most frequently cited work in the clinical vs. actuarial prediction debate. Meehl was an ardent proponent of statistical research methods and demonstrated, through exhaustive research, its superiority over clinical judgment.

Prediction lies at the heart of specialized professionals in all fields. Psychologists must make many clinical decisions, including treatment selection for patients. Meehl's work focused specifically on practical situations where psychologists needed to make predictions immediately. They could use the available data to make decisions based on their experience, training, and intuition or through statistical analysis. Meehl believed that whichever method generated the most accurate prediction in the long term should be the method employed.

In *Clinical Versus Statistical Prediction*, Meehl studied psychiatrists who must make predictions on the uncertain and complex behavior of psychiatric patients. Examining twenty different empirical studies, the statistics-based predictions were found to be superior to varying degrees. Further, there were over fifty research studies during that time that confirmed his findings (Meehl, 1965). More recently, Grove et al. were able to verify Meehl's findings through a meta-analysis using more robust statistical methods.[66] Analyzing a wider range of data and applying more rigorous meta-analytic techniques, the researchers found that mechanical prediction methods were 10 percent more accurate than clinical judgment. In 33–47 percent of the cases, mechanical methods were significantly more accurate; whereas 6–16 percent of the time, they were less accurate.

Echoing the conclusions of behavioral finance researchers, Meehl believed that the "problems of observation" are responsible for the inferiority of intuitive reasoning in prediction problems: "An obvious hypothesis, suggested by such researches as those of S. G. Estes (**40**) and the mass of material gathered by the Gestalt psychologists, is that the brain's 'superiority' shows up heavily at the level of perception itself. At the level of subtle cues of a primarily social type, any normal person has had a very long history of rewards and punishments with respect to responses to such cues. Responses to certain configurations of sense data as being indicators of the inner states of other organisms are presumably acquired very early."[67]

As discussed in chapter 3, the manner in which decisions regarding risk and reward are made was brilliantly captured by prospect theory. In short, the deductive reasoning involved in calculating the odds and payout is unnatural to the human brain. More relevantly, it is the reason computers were invented—so that human cognition could focus on the areas it *is* good at. Perhaps in another thousand years, the human brain will

---

66 W. M. Grove, D. H. Zald, A. M. Hallberg, B. Lebow, E. Snitz, and C. Nelson, "Clinical versus mechanical prediction: A meta-analysis," *Psychological Assessment* (2000).

67 Paul E. Meehl, *Clinical versus Statistical Prediction—A Theoretical Analysis and a Review of the Evidence* (Minnesota: The University of Minnesota Press, 1954).

evolve to accommodate the efficient deductive skills of the computer. Until then, intuitive judgment will always have a difficult time with uncertainty.

FUNDAMENTAL ANALYSIS IS FLAWED

Fundamental analysis assumes a causal connection between fundamental factors and its derivative security, which simply does not exist (e.g., company performance for a stock price or the economy for market averages). Any experienced trader knows that markets react to new events—but not in any way that makes sense. But these are supposedly merely short-term effects; even some system traders believe that "ultimately, the markets follow fundamentals."[68] The basic rationale is that eventually market prices reach their "fundamental" or "intrinsic" value, as reflected by economic laws, such as supply and demand.

However, as this section will show, the market and its fundamentals exist separate and distinct from one another. Market fundamentals are but one among many changing factors that determine market prices. In fact, the factors that *cause* market prices come from within the market itself; as such, there is no predetermined price toward which fundamentals drive. That is, there is no such thing as a fundamental price.

More pertinently, because fundamentals have such little bearing on markets, fundamental factors have no predictive power in market prices. Reliance on fundamental analysis cannot form the basis of any rational investment method and will inevitably lead to investment losses.

EXOGENOUS VS. ENDOGENOUS CAUSE

Many people insist upon being given 'reasons' for market action, both anticipated and actual, other than those derived from market analysis. However, conditions and events outside the market that are presumed to *cause* market trends in fact *lag* those trends. [69]

Consider for a moment what the market would look like if the markets followed economic events in the direct linear way many assume. The market would go sideways, waiting for some event. Once the event occurred, the market would immediately go to a certain price point, reflecting the new fundamental or intrinsic value. Upon the start of a war, the leading indices would immediately plummet and then immediately rise upon the end of the war. A company releasing a bad earnings report would be punished with a lower stock price immediately upon release. A decline in interest rates would send markets soaring upon the announcement of the rate decision.

---

68   Van K. Tharp, *Trade Your Way to Financial Freedom* (New York: McGraw-Hill, 2007).
69   Robert R. Prechter, *At the Crest of the Tidal Wave* (Hoboken, NJ: John Wiley & Sons, 1995).

Of course, the markets do not move in such fashion. Most of the time, the markets move with no relation to fundamentals; sometimes the markets move opposite to fundamentals. Perhaps investors need a psychologically soothing reason to buttress their investment beliefs. Paraphrasing from the thorough research of Robert Prechter of Elliott Wave International and The Socionomics Institute, a brief overview of four common myths will help highlight the flaws in common investment assumptions.

Myth #1: A strong economy makes the stock market go up.

If the economy is doing well, companies will do well. People will buy stocks and the stock market will go up. Nothing could make more sense. If the market was simple, rather than complex, perhaps it would work this way. In fact, it does not. Many times the market will go up while the GDP is low, and the market will go down while the GDP is strong.

If you knew ahead of time that next quarter's GDP would be the highest over the past sixteen years, would you buy stocks? This quarter was the fourth quarter of 1987. Yes, the big October crash of 1987, punctuated by a 22 percent decline in the Dow Jones Industrial Average on Black Monday, October 19.

Table 1 examines the increases in the S&P 500 three months and six months after a large increase in the quarterly GDP. With a few exceptions, large increases in the GDP do not lead to significant gains in the stock market.

Large Increase in GDP		Increase in S&P 500	
		3 months	6 months
Jan-84	3.23%	-2.06%	-5.87%
Oct-80	4.67%	1.63%	2.52%
Apr-74	5.84%	3.98%	-7.48%
Jan-76	3.38%	7.70%	1.77%
Jan-73	3.77%	-7.81%	1.12%
Jan-71	4.31%	8.42%	-8.05%
Jan-66	3.12%	-1.96%	-8.19%
Jan-55	3.39%	3.63%	14.65%
Oct-52	3.60%	7.59%	-6.67%
Jan-51	5.01%	3.55%	-1.30%

Table 1. GDP Increases vs. S&P 500 Index Price Change

Myth #2: Strong earnings make a stock go up.

Nothing could make more sense than the strong performance of a company causing its stock price to go up. But there is no evidence of this claim. Much of the research published by securities companies is based on corporate earnings analysis. The problem is that they never tell investors about the cases when this analysis is wrong, even though there is so much evidence. Investors never hear about the stock that went down because of low earnings. Stocks picks can then be culled from those with both strong earnings and increasing share prices.

Table 2 shows the S&P 500 index increases one year following a yearly increase in S&P 500 earnings. Here, too, there is no evidence that an increase in earnings causes the market to go up.

	Large Year-Over-Year Increases in S&P 500 Earnings	Increase in S&P 500 One Year After
2004	23.75%	3.00%
2002	18.51%	26.38%
1999	16.74%	-10.14%
1993	28.89%	-1.54%
1988	50.37%	27.25%
1984	26.71%	26.33%
1973	29.01%	-29.72%
1965	11.35%	-13.09%

Table 2. S&P 500 Earnings Increases vs. S&P 500 Index Price Change

Further, as seen in Table 3, the S&P 500 tends to do the exact opposite of common wisdom.

	Declines in S&P 500 Earnings	Increase in S&P 500 One Year After
2009	-4.59%	12.78%
2008	-20.78%	23.45%
2001	-30.79%	-23.37%
1991	-14.79%	4.46%
1982	-8.96%	17.27%
1975	-17.54%	19.15%
1970	-9.67%	10.79%

Table 3. S&P 500 Earnings Declines vs. S&P 500 Index Price Change

Myth #3: Lower interest rates make the stock market go up.

Bonds and stocks compete for investment capital. Hence, rising interest rates will make stocks less attractive and cause capital flows into bonds. Lower interest rates make stocks more attractive. Sounds reasonable. If only the markets actually behaved this way, the Fed would be able to manipulate the markets at will, and there would never be market crashes. Here is an example of plummeting interest rates coinciding with a market crash.

Table 4 tells a similar story: lower interest rates do not lead to higher stock prices.

	Decline in Interest Rate (10-Year Treasury)	Increase in S&P 500 One Year After
2008	-20.37%	23.45%
2001	-16.75%	-23.37%
1998	-17.17%	19.53%
1995	-7.06%	20.26%
1993	-16.26%	-1.54%
1986	-27.68%	2.03%
1985	-14.63%	14.62%
1983	-14.54%	1.40%
1976	-4.76%	-11.50%
1971	-16.19%	15.63%
1960	-58.30%	-11.81%

Table 4. Declines in Ten-Year Treasury
Rates vs. Increases in S&P 500 Index Price Change

Myth #4: Political events drive the stock market.

Analysts and market commentators routinely discuss geopolitical events to explain stock price movements. Dramatic political events may affect the markets temporarily. But what is the magnitude of such an effect? Is it something one can profit from? Do peaceful times cause markets to go up due to the peace and stability?

In fact, socionomics argues rather convincingly that a bad market will cause wars: "much like economic slumps, most wars *follow* the onset of bear markets, usually erupting late within them or shortly thereafter."[70] More precisely, a negative social mood will cause markets to go down. Markets are far more sensitive as they are more liquid. They therefore act as leading indicators of social mood. Wars usually occur toward the end of a long-term stock market downtrend, as wars are the last form of expression of negative social mood. Look at the following charts and examine the timing of wars in relation to the trend of the stock market.

For a far more comprehensive analysis of market myths of this type, please see www.elliottwave.com and www.socionomics.net. Chapter 4's discussion of the market as a complex adaptive system makes a controversial assumption. It assumes that all market behavior stems from forces within the market itself. This endogenous account of the market is at odds with the exogenous assumption of fundamental investing. This assumption underlies so much of economics and finance, but, appallingly, there is no evidence for it.

---

70   Alan Hall, "Global Market Perspective," *Elliott Wave International* (2008).

THE FLAWS OF NEOCLASSICAL ECONOMICS

Much of fundamental investing's core assumptions originate in neoclassical economics (NE). In the simple, linear world of NE, where all investors are rational, efficient processors of all efficiently delivered information, markets are sure to revert to their fundamental values. Indeed, the idea that markets behave in an orderly manner, reflecting sound economic laws, is an appealing one. It is wrong, but unfortunately, the majority of investors still cling to its assumptions.

Much has been written in the past few years about the failures of NE. Its main criticism is that NE is a normative model as opposed to prospect theory, a descriptive model that explains how things happen in the real world. NE is an umbrella term that encompasses various schools of economic thought. Three basic assumptions permeate NE:

1) Rational Agents
2) Independent Action based on Perfect Information
3) The Market as a Pricing Mechanism

Rational Agents The first part of this book demonstrated, from various angles, that people are not rational. Their behavior is decidedly irrational. It is worth repeating, because if investors do not act rationally in the markets, fundamental reasons for market movements lose their causal effect. If a company's earnings and structural performance are above that of its peers, then rational investors would buy it until its share prices reflected its ability to generate greater profits. If lower interest rates made it cost -effective to take on a mortgage, rational home buyers would buy more houses.

As Prechter has shown irrational agents turn the causal arrow around when it comes to fundamentals and the markets. A rising market would indicate to rational agents that it is time to expand, ride the trend and, generally, be optimistic; however, it is increasingly optimistic people that make the stock market rise. Rather than recessions causing businessman to be cautious (as rational businessmen would), cautious businessmen cause recessions from their overly cautious behavior. It is not the availability of derivatives that cause people to speculate, but rather a desire to speculate that causes the development of derivatives.[71]

Independent Action Examples of herding behavior are plentiful throughout economies and the markets. The examples in chapter four demonstrate that economic agents and traders do not act independently of each other with perfect information. Even with abundant sources of information, agents tend to take cues from other agents around them either because of a lack of confidence or due to a lack of information. Either way, herding causes agents to buy into each other's decisions and create what econophysi-

---

71 Robert Prechter, "Elliott Wave Theorist," *Elliott Wave International* (September 17, 2004).

cists call information cascades.

Bikhchandani, Hirshleifer, and Welch define an information cascade as a phenomenon wherein "individuals, having observed the actions and possibly payoffs of those ahead of them, take the same action regardless of their own information signals. Informational cascades may realize only a fraction of the potential gains from aggregating the diverse information of many individuals, which helps explain some otherwise puzzling aspects of human and animal behaviour."[72]

Information cascades have been found by researchers in a wide range of fields, from political upheavals to advertising. The Kirman example in chapter 4 of herding behavior in ants shows that information cascades, whether about the existence of a food source or the belief that the stock market will crash, attracts the majority—for example, 80 percent of the ants in the colony—into one direction that pushes the system into unstable conditions. Complexity theory shows that such behavior is intrinsic to many different types of adaptive systems. Ironically, because it pays to acquire knowledge from others (rather than discovering it for oneself), information cascade behavior is considered rational (one of the many logical inconsistencies with NE).

Price Mechanism The importance of price is shared by system traders, technical analysts, and, surprisingly, neoclassical economists. The difference is in its conception and history. NE believes that the market price reflects a fundamental price, which is the result of supply and demand aggregation driven by rational agents trying to maximize utility. Hence, exogenous forces—that is, economic fundamentals—are key to determining this price. If the API reports that unleaded gasoline supplies have dropped, rational agents would instantly update prices by buying gasoline.

Price plays a more central role, as it provides the basis for an equilibrium point, which will be discussed in the next section. To repeat, the behavioral economic, econophysical, and complexity models discussed in chapter 4 demonstrate that market prices (given autonomous agents interacting with each other) do not fix upon one market price. Although theoretically nice, the NE model of well-behaved agents fixing upon a fundamental price is purely hypothetical. Realistic simulations show that behaviors become far more complex. More importantly, they show that market prices are generated from the inner workings of the markets themselves. That is, *there is no fundamental price*, only a market price.

---

72 Sushil Bikhchandani, David A. Hirshleifer, and Ivo Welch, "Information Cascades," in *The New Palgrave Dictionary of Economics* (London: Palgrave Macmillan/U.K., 2008).

ECONOMIC EQUILIBRIUM

In addition to these three assumptions, equilibrium is another erroneous assumption held by NE. Eric Beinhocker does a wonderful of job of explaining the *historical* development of economic equilibrium in the second chapter of *The Origin of Wealth*.

Leon Walras is considered the author of NE's conception of market equilibrium. In an attempt to conform to simple mathematics and make economic phenomena predictable, Walras makes key assumptions that idealize the pricing mechanism. Unfortunately, "Walras's willingness to make trade-offs in realism for the sake of mathematical predictability would set a pattern followed by economists over the next century."[73]

Walras's first assumption is that the any market has one equilibrium point that could be calculated mathematically. The result is the fundamental price point on which that market would inevitably settle, based on current supply and demand. To calculate this equilibrium point, Walras coopted a model used by a contemporary physicist. The problem here is that the underlying model itself was a work in progress that was far from complete.

Paraphrasing Beinhocker, NE's equilibrium model is missing the second law of thermodynamics, incorporating only the first. By fixing its parameters (rational agents, utility maximization) and its quantities (goods, participants), the first law guarantees equilibrium. The concepts of economic scarcity and the impossibility of wealth creation all stem from the need to fix quantities at the outset. Nothing can be added to the system once in play (one reason fundamental analysis during the dot-com era seemed especially out of place).

The second law of thermodynamics introduced the idea of entropy, the force continuously driving systems into a state of disorder. Of course, entropy was still being formulated a hundred years after Walrus. Hence, Walras's model is largely deficient and caused NE to misclassify the economy as a closed system. A knowledge of the second law and its implications might have led to a more realistic, open system model.

As an open system, the economy is continually drawing in new sources of ideas, energy, and value from as many different sources as it can. These new inputs work against entropy to create order in the form of ideas, products, services, and organizations. More specifically, as a complex adaptive system, the economy employs all the tricks and tools of natural evolution to generate innovation and growth.

The Santa Fe Artificial Stock Market demonstrates this distinction quite clearly. With no evolutionary forces driving trading agents to learn (simulating a closed system), the market settles to stable price points. With an open setting that drives traders to learn, adapt, and evolve, it displays the characteristics of a real market. In other words, an open system is a far better representation of what is seen in the real world.

Hence, predicting an equilibrium price point (i.e., the fundamental price) using fundamental analysis of appropriate supply and demand factors is a fool's errand. In fact, if

---

73 Ibid.

the open and adaptive characteristics of the economy were correctly accounted for, it would become immediately clear that *there is no fundamental price.*

SUMMARY

Brian Arthur, in *Positive Feedbacks in the Economy*, discusses the way the VHS overtook the Beta format in the VCR market. He explains that increasing returns (as opposed to diminishing returns) or positive feedback loops took small, initial differences and magnified them to create a powerful trend for VHS adoption that drove beta out of business:

> Both systems were introduced at about the same time and so began with roughly equal market shares; those shares fluctuated early on because of external circumstances, "luck", and corporate maneuvering. Increasing returns on early gains eventually tilted the competition towards VHS: it accumulated enough of an advantage to take virtually the entire VCR market. Yet it would have been impossible at the outset of the competition to say which system would win, which of the two possible equilibria would be selected. Furthermore, if the claim that Beta was technically superior is true, then the market's choice did not represent the best economic outcome.[74]

In a similar fashion, many trends exhibited in markets develop due to endogenous market mechanisms (herding, information cascades, self-organized criticality). In spite of the curiosity of most investors, there are no explicit, singular causes for any type of market movement. Investing while looking for such causes or employing a strategy based on this line of reasoning will leave one far behind on most trends.

Fundamental investors would have been betting on one of either VHS or Beta, hiring analysts to evaluate consumer preferences, conduct market analyses, and so on. However, the eventual dominance of VHS was initially due to random factors, which could not have been foreseen. In fact, many analysts at the time were predicting Beta would win because of its technical superiority.

In the end, all of the initial fundamental research was worthless. Most fundamental analysis is done in exactly the same manner, but *it does not translate into accurate market predictions.* Fundamental analysis is, in essence, based on a two-hundred-year-old, partially developed physical model that cannot model basic market phenomena.

In sum, fundamental investing suffers from three serious flaws, which the previous chapters have (hopefully) demonstrated. First, investors are irrational and do not follow rational principles that maximize payouts or happiness; they certainly do not follow

---

74 Brian Arthur, "Positive Feedbacks in the Economy," *Scientific American* (1990).

economic laws. Investors generally will not buy undervalued stocks or sell overvalued stocks and do not recognize any kind of fundamental value.

Second, the economic laws and models on which fundamental analysis are founded are far too distant from the markets to have any predictive value. Markets have a life of their own, driven by endogenous forces. The common exogenous causes analyzed by fundamental investors are but one irregularly applied factor among many in the markets' decentralized structure. Moreover, markets often lead economic phenomena.

Finally, real markets are not closed off with fixed quantities that seek a balance between supply and demand. As attractive as such an equilibrium point may be, there is simply no fundamental price toward which a market is headed. That renders concepts such as "value investing," "intrinsic value," "overvalued," and "undervalued" meaningless. Markets generate prices of their own accord, and these prices are in a constant state of flux, going from stable to unstable as markets adapt to continuously changing conditions.

WHY FUNDAMENTAL DISCRETIONARY INVESTING IS NOT RATIONAL

In spite of recent failures, governments, large corporations, and the majority of the world's capital are managed with methods based on fundamental analysis and neoclassical economics. It is hoped that the proponents of this approach will someday go the way of astrologers and witch doctors. Until then, the market will continue to punish those who do not heed its own signals. Moreover, the market will always favor those with a rigorous, scientific method of processing market knowledge.

Scientific methods continue to face stiff resistance at all levels of society, throughout many industries. The scientific method has been around for centuries, and yet the majority of people believe that it belongs exclusively in the sciences. But the scientific method is a method of inquiry, for gathering data and acquiring knowledge. In spite of its shortcomings, it is the best method by which to separate fact from fiction.

While discretionary investing suffers from the flaws of intuition in calculating risk and uncertainty, fundamental analysis suffers from its false assumptions about the economy. A rigorous, scientific approach to studying investing (decision making), the economy, and markets would solve these problems. This section examines the underlying logical flaws of fundamental analysis.

FLAWED REASONING

The majority of discretionary investing (including the technical variety) consists mainly of piling on confirmatory evidence. These reasons, causes, or indicators may or may not be correlated. Once there is "enough" evidence, the investment decision is initiated. Using this approach, the investor can easily be overcome by confirmation bias. This is why the scientific approach called *verification* has been discredited.

VERIFICATION VS. FALSIFIABILITY

Verification was created with the best of intentions. Philosophers of the Vienna Circle wanted a better way to separate truth from falsehood. They proposed that the only truths that can be known are those which can be verified empirically, that is, through scientific experimentation. In its bare form, verification only requires one instance where A = B, to establish its truth.

The fallacy with verification is called *affirming the consequent*. In formal logic, verification would be represented thus:

If P, then Q
Q
Therefore, P

This argument is invalid, because P can be true without Q being true. For example,

If I take this sleeping pill, I will go to sleep.
I went to sleep.

Therefore, I took the pill.
There could be many other explanations for why I am sleeping, including the possibility that I am sleepy (but did not take the pill).

Another example:

If God created the universe, there would be order in nature.
There is order in nature.
Therefore, God created the universe.

Evolution and complexity theory offer alternative explanations for order (other than intelligent design) in nature. One cannot conclude that God created the universe from the two premises.

Or, more pertinently:

If the fundamental value of stocks is high, the economy is strong.
The economy is strong.
Therefore, the fundamental value of stocks is high.

It is further reasoned that if stock prices are low, they are undervalued, and, hence, an investor should buy. Aside from premise 1 being false, it does not follow that stocks will go up because of the strength of the economy. There are many alternate reasons for stocks going up.

Further, the fallacy in verification cannot be overcome by establishing more causes for the same conclusion. They each suffer from the same logical fallacy. Many investors reason that a strong economy, plus a favorable government administration, plus the company's competitive strengths each add the stock's chances of appreciating. But such a collection of fallacious causes only creates confirmation bias, making one's investment success only *appear* more likely.

To note, verification's underlying process of intuitive hypothesizing or inductive reasoning is an important one. But it serves its function in *discovering* facts about the world, not verifying or confirming them. Hume was its biggest skeptic, asserting that causal relationships inferred from observations were a psychological byproduct and reflected nothing of the real world. Hume claimed that, as far a logical correctness dictates, no amount of observed instances could prove an inductive hypothesis, as could a valid deductive argument.

VALID REASONING

Karl Popper's main contribution to the philosophy of science was the insight that science cannot prove anything true—it can only prove things false. In other words, although many instances cannot verify a hypothesis, one instance can negate it. Popper concluded that science must restrict itself only to that which could be falsified. That is, true scientific knowledge is that which, after tests, cannot be falsified. Even then, this theory would only be provisionally true, as one may find evidence to negate the theory in the future, at which point it would be falsified.

Logically, falsification takes the following valid argument:

P then Q
not Q
Therefore, not P

This argument is called *modus tollens* and is defined as *denying the consequent*. It is logically valid, as opposed to verification's affirming the consequent argument.

Here is an example:

If God created the universe, there would be order in nature.
There is no order in nature.
Therefore, God did not create the universe.

It is logically impossible for God to have created the universe if premise 1 is true, and there is no order in nature.

Hence, evidence cannot be used to verify a hypothesis due to its logically invalid form. However, evidence can be used to falsify a hypothesis. In other words, science proceeds by disqualifying false explanations and hypotheses and, on rare occasions, accepting those hypotheses for which there is no negative data as provisionally true.

It goes without saying that for a hypothesis to be falsifiable, it must first be in a testable form. "A good economy makes stocks go up" is not testable. "A statistically significant increase in an economy's GDP leads to a statistically significant increase in its main equity index for one month following the release of the GDP figures" is testable. One important implication is that there must be a *way* to test the hypothesis. Even with a great deal of financial data available to investors, fundamental investors continue to make hypotheses for which there is no test.

For example, during the dot-com bubble, the media was awash with bold predictions of how the new economy had made business cycles obsolete. Investors concluded that there were no constraints on the possible growth of dot-com businesses. A fun idea—but how would one go about testing this theory? Such pronouncements are nearly devoid of value and certainly should not form the basis of an investment strategy.

A trading system is testable to an extreme. Since computer-simulated backtesting is routinely used, every part of the strategy must be coded; there is no room for ambiguity. There is also an abundant supply of data with which to test; many of the commodities markets have over fifty years of historical data.

Even with statistical testing, to *verify* a hypothesis, one would have to be able to test for every single supporting claim. Testing all possibilities, including future ones, is obviously impossible. It is, however, possible to falsify a hypothesis with statistical analysis, because it only requires testing one claim. This formulation of the hypothesis that allows falsification is called the *null hypothesis*.

Mainstream science proceeds indirectly by describing an alternative hypothesis and a null hypothesis. The alternative hypothesis is the positive claim one is making, for example: "A statistically significant increase in an economy's GDP leads to a statistically significant increase in its main equity index for one month following the release of the GDP figures." Again, this claim is impossible to verify. Hence, one creates a null hypothesis, which is simply the negation of the alternative hypothesis.

The idea is to try to falsify the null hypothesis to prove the alternative hypothesis. The null hypothesis is the primary one, because science approaches all claims to knowledge with a skeptical attitude first; if its null hypothesis can be falsified, it can be accepted as a scientific theory. The null hypothesis of our example would be, "A statistically significant increase in an economy's GDP does *not* lead to a statistically significant increase in its main equity index for one month following the release of the GDP figures."

One way to test the alternative hypothesis would be to construct a backtest that would buy one S&P 500 futures contract on the day of an increase in the GDP and hold the position for one month. Consistent profits, using this strategy over a statistically valid sample of historical data comprising GDP figures and S&P 500 prices, would not prove the alternative hypothesis. However, an unprofitable backtest would falsify the alternative hypothesis. Testing the null hypothesis might provide valuable information.

The argument of the test would take the following form:

Alternative Hypothesis (AH): If there is a statistically significant increase in an economy's GDP, then (upon release of the GPD figures) the main equity index will increase by a statistically significant amount in the following month.

Null Hypothesis (NH): If there is a statistically significant increase in an economy's GDP, then (upon release of the GPD figures) the main equity index will *not* increase by a statistically significant amount in the following month.

Premise 1: If NH is true, then a backtest will be unprofitable.
Premise 2: A backtest was *not* unprofitable (it showed consistent profits).
Conclusion: NH is false, therefore AH is true.

If it was shown that the backtest was unprofitable, the second premise would be false, and therefore one would not be able to conclude that NH is false (and that AH is true). However, all it would take is one profitable backtest to conclude that NH is false. Because this test is of a statistical nature, issues such as sampling errors, data-mining biases, and overfitting must also be addressed before validating the results of the test.

The key point is that any claim made toward the predictability of market patterns should be viewed skeptically and tested rigorously, using the falsifiability procedure. And therein lies the basic logical flaw of discretionary fundamental investing: in most cases, there is no method that can be tested or falsified, which means it can never been proven to work. It can never be confirmed in any scientific way that discretionary fundamental investing has any predictive power or can generate profits.

SUMMARY

In chapter 2, four requirements were laid out with respect to a rational investment method:

1) Testable: all necessary and sufficient rules within system are clearly defined and integrated coherently
2) Clear objective
3) Evidence of efficacy: evidence that it is profitable (meets its objective/utility maximization)
4) Logical validity: method's core components must be logical valid

In sum, discretionary fundamental investing is an unfounded, invalid, and, ultimately, irrational approach to investing. In spite of its popularity, it fails to meet the first, third, and fourth requirements for rationality. Its discretionary nature makes it untestable. Most methods of fundamental investing are too vague in its formulations and, hence, are not testable. Further, most fundamental strategies only address possible reasons for entering the market. None of the other key components of a successful investment strategy are discussed: entry timing techniques (the "trigger" that initiates the trade), when to exit, and how much to invest (money management).

There is little evidence that fundamental analysis can predict market prices in a way that can lead to investment profits. Without evidence of a fundamental price, fundamental analysis is without merit and exhibits no predictive power. Finally, because of its amorphous nature, it cannot be falsified; therefore, there is no logical way to prove its efficacy. Any attempts to formulate the basic underlying reasoning will only expose its invalid logic. That is, discretionary fundamental investing lacks validity at all levels.

A rational approach to investing would start with assumptions that have been proven to be true of the markets, incorporating purely market-based signals that have predictive power and a systematic set of rules proven to generate statistically significant profits on a consistent basis. System trading is the one method that does meet these requirements.

PART III: RATIONAL INVESTMENT

CHAPTER 6. WHY SYSTEM TRADING?

WHAT IS SYSTEM TRADING?

WHAT IS IT?

Given the emotional and psychological obstacles and the irrationality of the markets, system trading is the most advantageous way to avoid these various pitfalls. More so, it is the only *rational* way to invest. So, what is system trading, exactly? In *Design, Testing and Optimization of Trading Systems*, Robert Pardo defines a trading system as "a mechanical means of trading systematically."[75]

It is mechanical rather than discretionary; hence, it provides clear entry and exit signals, with no judgment required at the time of execution. Thus, trading systems are not subject to the whims of the trader. The logic behind the strategy is quantified, so that there is no ambiguity as to what actions the trader should take. All strategic decisions are made prior to entering the market. It is also systematic, meaning that all core aspects of the trade—from entry to exit, which markets to trade and how much to trade—are all integrated into one complete system.

Systematically integrated thinking is at the core of rationality. Rationality has been defined as following an integrated set of principles that are logical and coherent—principles that, when followed, will maximize a specific outcome (e.g., a Calmar Ratio above 1.00). Thus, trading with a valid, profitable trading system in the pursuit of maximized profits is the very essence of rational investing.

A trading system usually uses technical based indicators and patterns (i.e., from the technical analysis domain). Technical indicators are quantitative and, hence, are easy to define and manipulate. Further, technical analysis does not seek to understand *why* the market is going up; it only seeks to show that there is some evidence that it is likely to go up. As discussed in the previous chapter, fundamental analysis is deficient for understanding the workings of the market. Most importantly, there are no proven cause-and-effect relationships between the economy and the markets. Hence, although there have been attempts to develop trading systems based on fundamental analysis (of necessity, they were econometric models), the most successful ones have primarily been of the technical variety.

CLEARLY DEFINED

Before one can even begin to test a prediction or market theory, one must be able to articulate one's view in a statement that can be tested. Think about most of the

---

75 Robert Pardo, *Design, Testing and Optimization of Trading Systems* (Hoboken, NJ: Wiley, 1992).

views expressed by pundits and the media. "We believe the market will go up" is a vague statement with very little predictive content. How much will it go up? From when? Until when? How quickly? For a trader, such comments are not helpful. System trading in practice involves a great deal of coding and testing using historical data. Hence, the first requirement of a trading system is that it be clearly defined.

A clearly defined statement or strategy, then, is testable, the first requirement for a rational investment strategy. Most investment methods are problematic, because it is impossible to test whether this prediction is right or wrong. To make a clear prediction that can be tested and hence, add, definitively, to our knowledge, one must say something like, "We believe the S&P 500 will be up more than 10 percent by the end of the year." Right or wrong, it is something that can be verified at the end of the year, and the forecaster can be clearly evaluated as right or wrong.

For whatever reason, even experienced professionals resist attempts at quantifying their prognostications. In many cases, it belies a lack of understanding about the domain in question. The fact is, every investor has a model or strategy that expresses some world view, position, and, ultimately, a forecast about the markets. The only difference between these investors and a system trader is that the system trader has *made explicit* his forecast.

This difference is widespread and exists even in the sciences. In his paper "Why Model?" Epstein illuminates the distinction:

> The first question that arises frequently—sometimes innocently and sometimes not—is simply, "Why model?" Imagining a rhetorical (non-innocent) inquisitor, my favorite retort is, "You *are* a modeler." Anyone who ventures a projection, or imagines how a social dynamic—an epidemic, war, or migration—would unfold is running *some* model. But typically, it is an *implicit* model in which the assumptions are hidden, their internal consistency is untested, their logical consequences are unknown, and their relation to data is unknown. But, when you close your eyes and imagine an epidemic spreading, or any other social dynamic, you are running *some* model or other. It is just an implicit model that you haven't written down....[76]

> The choice, then, is not whether to build models; it's whether to build *explicit* ones. In *explicit* models, assumptions are laid out in detail, so we can study exactly what they entail. On these assumptions, *this* sort of thing happens. When you alter the assumptions *that* is what happens. By writing explicit models, you let others replicate your results. You *can*

---

76 Joshua Epstein, "Why Model?" *Journal of Artificial Societies and Social Simulation* (2008).

in fact calibrate to historical cases if there are data, and can test against current data to the extent that exists. And, importantly, you can incorporate the best domain (e.g., biomedical, ethnographic) expertise in a rigorous way. Indeed, models can be the focal points of teams involving experts from many disciplines.[77]

Vague prognostications are so common, one might wonder whether the bulk of market forecasts are intentionally ambiguous—that is, they are made to avoid accountability. Whatever the motivations may be, most market forecasts are like astrological predictions, to which Daniel Dennett has remarked: "When astrological predictions come true this is sheer luck, or the result of such vagueness or ambiguity in the prophecy that almost any eventuality can be construed to confirm it."[78]

As reiterated throughout this book, using more common methods of observation and decision making are fine for common phenomena. It is during situations of uncertainty and complexity that scientific methods of analysis and decision making become absolutely necessary to avoid the pitfalls of biased cognition and ensure that genuinely verified patterns of behavior are found.

Market movements should, in general, be expressed in quantifiable, codable terms. "Uptrend" is better than "going up," because an uptrend actually has a clear definition: higher highs and higher lows. In computer code, this definition can be expressed as

Uptrend = high[N]>high[N-1] and low[N]>low[N-1].

Obviously, there are many varieties of trend; many of these can be defined precisely and coded for manipulation and testing. Other definitions of trend include the following:

Uptrend = high[N]>high[N-5] and low[N]>low[N-5]
Uptrend = high[N]>Moving Average and low[N]>Moving Average
Uptrend = Moving Average[short-term]>Long Moving [long-term]

POSITIVE EXPECTANCY

Prospect theory (PT) demonstrated the significant difference between the way people should think and the way they actually think. The normative model used to contrast PT with was the Expected Value Model (EVM). System traders use a simpler version of this model in evaluating possible trading systems, called *positive expectancy* (PE). Conformity to this model is one of the key reasons system trading can be counted on to produce rational strategies for investing.

---

77 Ibid.

78 Daniel Dennett, *The Intentional Stance* (Boston: MIT Press, 1987).

Winning is a vague concept in trading. Focusing on win% can severely hamper any trader; this is even more true with system traders. Although being right feels good, if the goal is to generate profits, PE is the goal. Good trend-following systems tend to have a low win% but a high win:loss ratio, resulting in profits. Good countertrend or range-based systems tend to have a high win% and a low win:loss ratio. Knowing when and where your system's profits come from is key to trading it successfully.

Positive expectancy (PE) is simply (win% * average win)-(loss% * average loss). So a good trend-following system may have a 40 percent win% with an average win of $2,500, along with a 60 percent loss% with an average loss of $800. The PE, then, is (0.40 * $2,500)-(0.60 * $800), or $470. Imagine the perfect system—which everybody would love to trade—that is right 90 percent of the time, winning $1 per winning trade, while losing $50 per losing trade (0.90 * $1)-(0.10 * $50)=-$4.10. Many discretionary investors have this type of profile. The lure is that being right 90 percent of the time, the investor spends most of his or her time winning, feeling great. The one big loss that comes along infrequently is usually rationalized away (another use of neoclassical economic models).

PE is the same as mathematical edge. A system that has an edge mathematically will eventually profit, regardless of the short-term fluctuations in performance. Indeed, trend-following systems are among the most successful of trading strategies. They have a long option profile (low win% and high payout). Venture capital and many entrepreneurial activities have the same profile. It is not uncommon for a trend-following system with a positive expectation to lose seven to eight times in a row and then break even with the profits from the next two trades.

Proprietary trading desks are often managed by executives who do not understand the importance of PE. Without such a framework, it is easy to judge initial

Once you start trading a system you have worked hard to develop, just trade it. We humans have built-in mechanisms to make rash decisions, so even if your losses are racking up, stick with it for a while.

Toby Crabel, a multibillion-dollar CTA and a legend in the system trading industry, has mentioned how some of his losing systems are kept alive, because some long-term systems go through one or two years of losing periods, only to become profitable for several years. He also admonishes system traders never to make changes to a system during drawdowns.

The logic makes sense, as even a breakeven system (zero positive expectations) will have its winning periods. Wait for these, and then figure out what is going on with the system.

When you analyze the system thus, after accumulating some (expensive) feedback on its performance, you can, at the very least, have some certainty about the validity of the system. Knowing a system is horrible and should never be traded is better than wondering if the system might work or not.

losses as a symptom of bad trading. Often, they simply cannot bear the pain of losing. But losses are necessary costs of doing business; they are akin to Cost of Goods Sold. In order to "try out" a trend, a small amount must be risked. It is well worth the risk—without this risk, there would never be profits. Put another way: losses from a valid trading system are the gross costs, with the trading profits being gross revenue. No business-person would expect gross revenue with incurring gross costs.

MARKET PATTERNS

Analyzing complex adaptive systems is a new field—still a work in progress. Traditional inductive analysis techniques fail miserably. Because the causes are unknown or too numerous, simple cause-and-effect models have little predictive value. What CASs do generate consistently are emergent patterns. Markets are no different, and the field of technical analysis is highly effective at identifying these patterns.

Because patterns in the market come exclusively from the market, technical analysis is more aptly termed *market analysis* or *endogenous pattern analysis*. These patterns emerge from traders interacting with other traders and the forces inherent in complex adaptive systems, such as feedback loops. As Arthur and Holland's trading agents demonstrated, technical analysis is as much a natural strategy as it is an emergent property.

Technical analysis is a study of the market itself and where its fundamental price is only that which traders decide with their buying and selling. In spite of the competing interests of the myriad traders, the market is not purely *random*; it is *complex*. There are movements and patterns that appear with regularity. As demonstrated in chapter 4, networks, self-organization, and herding all contribute to recognizable, repeatable market behavior.

Thus, human emotions and psychology expressed through the constraints of the market create consistent patterns of market behavior that traders can exploit for profits. The analysis of this behavior is the essence of technical analysis. Further, objective market analysis, the kind that can be integrated into a valid trading system, only seeks to find the condition of the market and make probabilistic predictions. *Why* the market is going up is not important; indications that the market *is* going up are important. A trader must focus on how to spot them early enough and exit them properly to profit from these signals.

Market patterns are usually found accompanied by larger market environments. Smart system traders are clear about which environments they seek to make money in. For every system, there will usually be one environment that will make the most profits, one environment that will make smaller profits, another that generates small losses, and a fourth that will cause large losses. Combined, a good system will average profits over the long term. However, all strategies, methods, and systems implicitly or explicitly target one type of environment, with the goal being to maximize profits in the favorable environments and to limit losses in the adverse ones.

Implicitly, there is no Holy Grail system that can make money in all market environments. All profitable systems will have bad days. They will have drawdowns—once in a while, they will have severe drawdowns. Positive expectancy, however, means that eventually they will recover and become profitable again. Market environments cycle through major modes of movement, although always in slightly different forms than before. For profitable systems, adverse market environments are what cause losses; as favorable environments cycle back, profits start to accrue again.

As a complex adaptive system, the market will continue to churn out new patterns within new environments that look like old ones but with slight mutations. Nonetheless, characterizing the market with four major states is useful. Curtis Faith, an original Turtle, wrote a great book on system trading titled *Way of the Turtle*. In it he discusses four primary "market states":

[S]peculative markets exist in one of four states:

— **Stable and quiet:** Prices tend to stay within a relatively small range with little movement up or down outside that range.

— **Stable and volatile:** There are large daily or weekly changes, but without major changes over a period of months.

— **Trending and quiet:** There is slow movement or drift in prices when measured over a period of months but without sever retracement or price movement in the opposite direction.

— **Trending and volatile:** There are large changes in price accompanied by occasional significant shorter-term reversals of direction.

Stable and quiet markets seem to be a bit rarer these days, but these states tend to make up the majority of markets. Both stable and volatile markets tend to occur during major economic news releases or events. Countertrend systems do well during these types of markets. Mean-reversion strategies profit highly, as the lack of trends keep losses infrequent. Trending and quiet markets are where many trend-following systems profit the most. The lack of volatility keeps whipsaw losses (where protective stop loss orders are triggered) few, and the smooth price action allows for an efficient exit. Finally, trending and volatile exits are difficult markets, but volatility-based, trend-following systems that enter on retracements can work in these markets.

RULE-BASED STRATEGIES

Most of the systems traded successfully are linear statistical models akin to the actuarial formulas discussed in chapter 5. Systems can be as simple as the Goldberg rule, with one formula and a threshold level that triggers entries and exits. For example, a simple moving average can be used to indicate the market trend. If the current close is above the moving average, then investors should buy and hold. If the market closes below the moving average, then investors should close the long position, initiate a short position, and hold.

> If close>MA, then (close short) buy.
>
> If close<MA, then (close long) sell.

This simple system can be tested on historical data, providing performance results by which to judge the system.

Successful systems tend to be more complicated, with two or three different indicators; some indicators can exhibit considerable sophistication with abilities to ascertain more subtle aspects of the market condition. Time and volume filters can be added. Risk management rules, such as stop-loss orders and profit-taking orders, are routinely used as well. More complicated systems are not necessarily better; in fact, they can lead to serious problems, as will be discussed in the following chapter. What these systems are not is complex. They are linear systems, and there are no emergent properties. They can be tested with common statistical analysis (backtesting).

Although the variety of successful systems is vast, conventional trading systems tend to have the following basic components:

1) Setup conditions
2) Entry rules
3) Entry filters
4) Exit rules
5) Risk management rules
6) Money management rules

1) Setup conditions define the specific market pattern or condition the system is targeting. Many times this part is incorporated into the entry rules. But it is useful to separate the two, if only to clarify what type of movement the system should profit from. For example, some traders believe that the strongest trends emerge from tight, congested patterns. Hence, the system can be "activated" once the market goes into a small range. Pseudo-code:

> If range of past 25 days < range of past 100 days, then go to next condition.

In many backtesting programs, codes can specify under which conditions the system is activated. If the above condition is true on the current bar, the program will then read the next set of conditions. If the ten-day range is the same or larger than that of the past one hundred days, the program will not recognize the above code as true and will move on to the next bar, starting from the beginning.

2) Entry rules are where the bulk of system development is spent. Although all parts of the system should not be neglected, entry rules do have a greater importance to the success of the system. The classic entry rule for trend-following systems is a breakout of the Donchian channel (created by Richard Donchian and popularized by the Turtle traders).

Pseudo-code:

If close>highest close of the past 10 days, then buy.

If close<lowest close of the past 10 days, then sell.

This type of rule is often called a trigger, as it contains the order to enter the market. 3) To increase the effectiveness of the system, filters can be added to avoid noise. In a trend-following system, volatile range markets can trigger entries, only to be followed by quick losses (whipsaws). A common filter is the Bollinger band. Because the bands adjust to short-term spikes outside the Donchian channel, it can filter out some of the whipsaws in the market. This filter can be added directly into the entry code.

Pseudo-code:

If close>upperband and close>highest close of the past 10 days, then buy.

If close<lowerband and close<lowest close of the past 10 days, then sell.

Filters can also be used to avoid undesirable market conditions, such as low volume. Placing orders only after market open where the liquidity is highest is a common filter.

Pseudo-code:

If current time>pit open and close>upperband and close>highest close of the past 10 days, then buy.

If current time>pit open and close<lowerband and close<lowest close of the past 10 days, then sell.

4) Exit rules are important, because they determine to what extent the system profits from a successful entry. High-percentage entries can only benefit a trader, if the exit rules are effective. For trend-following system, trailing stops are among the best. Although quite simple, moving averages are effective. Initially, the market may zigzag a bit before settling into a trend, a trailing stop is usually triggered upon some favorable move away from the entry.

Pseudo-code:
> If holding long position and current profit>$500 and close<moving average of 10 days, exit long position.

> If holding short position and current profit>$500 and close>above moving average of 10 days, exit short position.

5) Stop-loss orders are usually employed to manage risk. Hard-dollar stops are usually a bad idea, because varying volatility levels can trigger stops too often. Stop orders are commonly triggered upon indication that the trend has reversed. Hence, an effective stop can be constructed using a moving average or Bollinger band.

Pseudo-code:
> If holding long position and close<lower band, exit long position.

> If holding short position and close>upper band, exit short position.

One danger is that the Bollinger band may be too wide, and the stop order is so far away that outsized losses may be incurred. Hence, an additional filter is usually incorporated into the condition.

Pseudo-code:
> If (upper band-lower band)< $1,000 and holding long position and close<lower band, exit long position.

> If (upper band-lower band)< $1,000 and holding short position and close>upper band, exit short position.

This additional filter ensures that losses can never be greater than $1,000 per trade.
6) Money management rules determine how much will be risked and traded. In the futures markets, one trading unit is normally equal to one futures contract. The number of futures contracts traded determines leverage and results in profits and losses being multiplied. A common money management rule, or position-sizing rule, is to use the initial risk calculated above in the risk management rule. If a system risks 1 percent of capital each time it trades on a $100,000 account, $1,000 is available to risk. If the current hard-dollar amount difference between the upper and lower bands is $500, then two contracts will be traded. The advantage, of course, is that risk is limited, whereas profits are not.

With this system, the ideal set up is for an unusually small range to form. With a lower risk, more contracts can be traded. Once in the market, the system holds its position, following a trend that is unusually calm (low volatility) and, hence, not triggering the trailing stop. After the market has moved a significant amount, the market settles into a range, and the moving average catches up, triggering an exit at a good price. With a higher number of contracts traded, the total profit is several times the initial amount risked. Thus, the money management rule and the exit rule combine to generate asymmetric returns.

Successful systems take this general form but usually add a number of variations to give them an extra edge (positive expectation). Much more can be added as well, but a fully integrated system must have each of these components.

STATISTICAL INFERENCE

Much of the power of system trading comes from its ability to test a strategy on historical data to demonstrate its effectiveness. Backtesting does not attempt to find causal links, as fundamental analysis does. It is looking for statistical relationships between *indicators* and *market patterns*. There is inherent uncertainty in these relationships; hence, modeling these relationships properly belongs in the domain of statistics and probability. Fortunately for traders, a system only needs to have *some* (not total) predictive power (since it can make more when it is right than losses when it is wrong).

Backtesting is based on statistical inference from sampling. This form of reasoning is used widely by researchers in many fields including the sciences. Its effectiveness in prediction is well documented, and its logical form is valid. Briefly, statistical inference is simply an attempt using statistical methods to generalize from historical data and extrapolate those generalizations into the future. The extrapolation is where the uncertainty lies, because the future will never look exactly like the historical data from which those generalizations were ascertained. By using historical data, backtesting is a form of sampling—the sample being the historical data. Once the sample ascertains a generalization or pattern, one can infer that it will hold into the future to some degree.

A typical research problem explores a sample of historical data to find evidence of predictive behavior. Typically, an alternate hypothesis asks the question, "Does being taller increase one's chances of getting a job?"[79] The statistical way to ask this question, given random effects that can mask true patterns or relationships, is: "Does this observed result really provide evidence that there is a real advantage for taller person over a shorter candidate….Is the high number due to a real height advantage or just due to chance?" Backtests would ask the question, "Are the profits shown by the backtest 'real,' or did the system just get lucky?"

The next step is to define the null hypothesis, as discussed in chapter 5. Here, the null hypothesis would be that there is no advantage in being taller and that the chances of a tall person being hired over an equally qualified shorter person is no greater than a coin toss. In other words, the taller person's chance over the short person should be roughly 50/50. However, due to random chance, even coin tosses can seem favorable to one side. That is, heads should come up 0.50 times, but in actuality, it can deviate from this number. So even if tall people could be hired 60 percent of the time, one could not

---

79

reject the null hypothesis. Sixty percent is only 0.10 more than 0.50, well within standard deviations.

Significant deviations are limited, however. The probability of heads appearing ten times out of thirteen tosses is less than 0.05. In fact, an occurrence with a probability of less than 0.05 would be, by convention, considered statistically significant, showing that such a phenomenon was very unlikely to happen. In other words, if sample data demonstrated such an occurrence, it could not be explained simply by luck; there is something for significant at work (a genuine edge or advantage). What this means is if data showed that taller candidates were hired over shorter candidates ten out of thirteen times, the null hypothesis would be rejected, and it would provide some evidence that there is an edge for being taller.

Similarly, if a backtest were to show minimal profits that were below the statistically significant level, one could not reject the null hypothesis (that the system's profits were due to luck); hence, one would have no evidence supporting the profitability of the trading system. Any positive expectation demonstrated by the backtest was just because the system got lucky. Conversely, if profits were high enough, such that the level of profitability had a less than 0.05 chance of happening, the null hypothesis would be rejected, and the system would likely be profitable in real-time trading.

Unfortunately, many system traders commit mistakes similar to those of discretionary fundamental investors in trying to confirm their system directly, from the outset. Instead of testing to reject the null hypothesis, they attempt to confirm the alternate hypothesis. Typically, indicators are added to the same historical data set until improvements are seen in the backtest performance. These traders are succumbing to confirmation bias and are not verifying anything. Instead, they are overfitting to historical data and making it impossible for the system to generalize to future data.

WHAT IS BACKTESTING?

Ensuring that the entire research and development procedure surrounding the backtest conforms to these statistical principles takes some skill and experience. Indeed, aside from executing trading systems, where a host of cognitive biases can prevent proper trading of systems, backtesting is where most system traders stumble. Without a firm grasp of statistical principles, correct research procedures, and a significant amount of experience, many traders start trading a system whose backtested performance looks great—but then generates losses when traded in real time. Today's wide availability of backtesting software has greatly commoditized an advanced, sophisticated verification tool, but all powerful tools require skillful users. The issues involved in correct backtesting procedures are many, and a number of them will be discussed in detail in chapter 7.

A basic backtest consists of the following core parts[80]:

1) Sufficient Data
2) Testing Procedures
3) Optimization
4) Proper Evaluation

SUFFICIENT DATA

Having more data is generally better. More data can provide better indications of the effectiveness of the system and provide more information about its performance characteristics. By increasing the sample size, a system can be tested on a greater number of possible future patterns. Standard error measures the accuracy of the backtest results. It is calculated using the number of trades the system generated in the backtest.

<formula>

where N is the number of trades (sample size). The more trades there are, the smaller the error. Hence, regardless of the length of the test data, what is important is the number of trades the backtest generates. One hundred trades generates a 10 percent standard error (<formula>). A 10 percent standard error means that if the system is shown to generate an average trade of $500, it will do so with an error of +/- $50, or from $450 to $500. This range is an acceptable difference, so a backtest over one hundred trades is ideal.

Degrees of freedom (DF) is discussed in more detail in the next chapter. The more rules in a trading system, the more constraints are placed on the data, restricting its DF. Roughly speaking, the more data in relation to the number of rules, the greater the DF. The greater the DF, the more reliable its results. One hundred trades may be enough for a simple system, but if those trades were generated on a specific type of pattern that dominated the data set, DF could be greatly diminished.

One way to avoid this problem is to examine the data set and ensure that it has a variety of market patterns. At minimum, the data set should contain both uptrends and downtrends, trends as well as ranges, and low and high price levels. Market spikes, sharp rebounds, high and low volatility, and different types of trends and ranges (steady, sharp) are good to include as well. The idea is to examine how the system handles the different types of patterns the market will throw at the system in real time.

---

80 This section is by no means a practitioner's guide to backtesting. The scope of the book is to outline the *rationale* for system trading. This section serves to simply define backtesting in theoretical terms.

TESTING PROCEDURES

Generally speaking, backtesting should involve several stages. Preliminary tests should determine whether the coding is correct and the system is trading the way it was meant to trade. The bulk of system development should be spent here, examining how the system responds to different types of markets. Traders are often surprised to find several unintended (and most bad) trades and go back to the coding stage to fine-tune the system. Before starting long simulations or optimization runs, a system trader wants to see some positive expectancy and profitable characteristics from the system.

During this phase, the range of each parameter should be roughly determined. If the system employs a short-term moving average, an appropriate range for the average period should be determined, for example, 5–20 bars (rather than 1–100). If the trader has a clear idea of the types of trends he or she is targeting, this part should be relatively easy. Still, initial testing should confirm the estimates.

Once this range is determined, the system should be optimized over that range. A good trading system will have several optimal parameter sets over the test data. More importantly, the performance should distribute normally over the parameter range. That is, if thirteen bars is determined to be the optimal moving average lookback period, twelve and fourteen bars should be similar, if slightly less profitable. Eleven and fifteen should be more so. The distribution should look like a bell curve. If looks like a cliff or a spike, the system is not generalizing well and should be scrapped.

Next, a series of out-of-sample (OOS) tests should be conducted to ensure there is no overfitting. OOS is covered extensively over the next two chapters. The system must be tested on data that it has not seen before. So, using an entirely new data set, the system should be tested. The results should be somewhat similar to the original backtested results. Usually, a series of OOS tests are conducted, and the results are averaged; this average is then compared to the original backtested results.

If these results are good, many traders will paper trade the system for a specified period of time. They trade the system on real-time data and record the results. In the author's experience, two or three out of ten rigorously verified systems will be filtered out in the final stage, due to a variety of reasons.

OPTIMIZATION

In practice, experienced system traders do much of the optimization during the development phase. As noted above, selecting a parameter set range is itself a first phase of optimization. Specifying the particular types of market patterns the system seeks to profit from will place constraints on the parameter range that facilitate the optimization process.

Optimization then becomes a matter of finding the best parameters for the trading system. Unfortunately, what most traders do is more akin to an exercise in combinatorics, as they see the parameter selection process as static—or worse, absolute. Optimization implies that there is a moving target of better values and that scientific procedures and tools will be used to search for them on an ongoing basis.

Hence, finding robust parameters, that is, parameters that work on a large set of data, is simply the optimal parameter set of that data. If different data is used, a different set of parameters is likely to be found. In other words, there is no single set of values that will be optimal continuously across the life of the system.

In essence, optimization is curve-fitting. We are looking for a set of values that will align better with the given data. Think of the system as a linear regression formula that is trying to fit the points of data represented by the backtesting historical data set. The parameters are the coefficients that allow for better fitting; this process is optimization.

The danger is in over-fitting, where the data fits too closely, giving up too much DF. Systems that are over-fitted to one set of data will not be able to generalize over other data. Hence, great backtest results lead to losses in real-time trading. Overfitting is an extremely difficult problem to tackle—and one that all traders experience. In nature, many species adapt too well to their environments, becoming kings of their realms, only to become extinct once changes in their environment make it hard for them to adapt.

PROPER EVALUATION

Backtested results should be evaluated with an eye to the system's future performance. In backtesting, some statistics are better than others in predicting the *future* performance of the system. Net profit and win percentage are generally poor, whereas risk-adjusted measures (e.g., Calmar Ratio) and a smooth equity curve are better.

What is most important in a trading system is that it turns the wild, leptokurtotic market into a series of consistent, stable, normally distributed equity streams. To the extent that a system has this ability (this varies widely from system to system), the system is more reliable and can be trusted to continue generating such performance into the future.

Given the inverse relationship between risk and return, good trading systems will lie somewhere between the extremes of a long-term, trend-following system and a high-frequency statistical arbitrage system. The former can generate excess returns for higher volatility (risk), whereas the latter can generate lower returns for lower volatility.

One good measure of a trading system is the K-Ratio, developed by Lars Kestner[81]:

K–Ratio = (Slope of Log VAMI Regression line) / ((Standard error of the slope)*(Number of period in the Log VAMI))

Simply, the K-ratio is a risk-adjusted measure of return, where the equity curve represents the return and the standard deviation of its slope measures risk. The greater is diverges, the greater the risk. The K-ratio can accommodate systems that generate profits slower or faster. But within that strategy, it rewards those that can do it in similar increments per unit of time.

Each experienced trader has his or her own favorites measures or they may use a different measure for different types of systems. Either way, the emphasis during backtesting should be placed on evaluating its future performance. In the next chapter, performance measures that place limits on performance will be discussed. These measures also contribute to predicting the stability of systems by lowering the risk of over-fitting.

WHY SYSTEM TRADING?

REDUCTIONISM - UNCOMFORTABLE THOUGHTS, PART II

In a well-designed system, the components are black boxes that perform their functions as if by magic. The faculty with which people ponder the world has no ability to peer inside itself or the other human faculties to see what makes them tick. That makes us the victims of an illusion: that our own psychology comes from some divine force or mysterious essence or almighty principle.

I want to convince you that our minds are not animated by some godly vapor or single wonder principle. The mind, like Apollo spacecraft, is designed to solve many engineering problems, and thus is packed with high-tech systems each contrived to overcome its own obstacles.

—Steven Pinker, *How the Mind Works*[82]

In spite of its proven success and its strong theoretical and empirical foundations, many in the investment community still reject system trading. This resistance seems to

---

81 Lars Kester, *Quantitative Trading Strategies* (New York: McGraw-Hill, 2003).
82 Steven Pinker, *How the Mind Works* (New York: W. W. Norton & Company, 1997).

be founded upon a deep-seated fear of system trading's mechanical nature. "Numbers are insufficient to capture the complicated workings of the real world" is a common complaint found in the sciences and represents discomfort towards reductionism.

Among the many great contributions of sociobiologists, such as Daniel Dennett, Steven Pinker, and Richard Dawkins, is the opening up of the many sacred cows in modern society and explicating their inner workings. In doing so, they have demonstrated that the forces of nature are algorithmic at their foundations, clearly definable and repeatable. Dennett discusses the engineering nature of biology in detail: "Darwin's great insight was that all the designs in the biosphere could be the products of a process that was as patient as it was mindless, an 'automatic' and gradual lifter in Design Space."[83]

This particular brand of evolution views all things in all life, from skyscrapers to iPads to the Amazon rainforest, as evolved through mechanistic processes. These processes are varied, complicated, and complex and work through a variety of cranes or tools, including skilled professionals, whose body of knowledge is passed on through verbal a variety of social mechanisms. However, this view—that all the most significant and important things were created by a mechanistic, algorithmic processes—is often seen as philistine, callous, or just extremely simplistic.

Even fundamental investors (who base their decisions on unfounded assumptions using incomplete physical models) feel that the quantitative approach of system trading is too simple, in that formulas cannot possibly capture all the nuances and complexities of the market. Thus, one of the primary barriers to system trading's adoption is this fear of or anxiety towards reductionism.

Reductionism is one of those ideological concepts that have become a silent fixture in modern culture. It has been around for a while now and continues to incite controversy. Much of the investment industry's aversion towards quantitative, algorithmic, mechanical, and any type of systematic trading stems from a fear of reductionism. How can something as interesting, special, complex, and difficult as investing be done with something so simple?

Reductionism is the general stripping down of a phenomenon into simpler parts—ultimately, down to its fundamental structure. Another way to characterize it would be to filter out the noise and bluster to see the phenomenon as it really is. Unfortunately, much of mainstream culture indoctrinates a general fear that all the warm, fuzzy, meaningful, inspiring things in the world will be explained away, leaving only a bare, mechanical, and boring world. Indeed, the very word "mechanical" has come to carry a negative connotation for this very reason.

Reductionism certainly does dispel many of the warm fuzzies; society loves to worship wise politicians, visionary business leaders, revolutionary innovations, the Oracle of Omaha. At the same time, reductionism also dispels a lot of the demons and devils;

---

83 Ibid.

throughout history, investors have blamed corrupt politicians,[84] program trading, short sellers, and speculators for market crashes. Dr. Richard Geist is much more articulate about this point:

> But our (investment) decisions, as we now know, are based on more than objective data. Every investment is accompanied by fantasies, conscious or unconscious, that embody our deepest experiences of being in the world....For example, we may believe that some new technology will change the way our culture does business; we may believe that a CEO is the smartest manager we've ever met, someone capable of leading his or her company to tremendous market share in his or her industry; or our financial analysis may lead us to conclude we've brilliantly discovered an undervalued investment opportunity.

> Think of the times you buy a stock and it immediately appreciates. Even if the transitory increase has nothing to do with the reasons you bought the stock, you feel smart and competent. Everyone who invested in the dot-com's before March 2000 felt like a brilliant investor to be admired and applauded for his stock-picking savvy. Those who believed in Henry Blodget or Mary Meeker and were guided by their analysis of some of the Internet stocks felt bolstered and uplifted by their imagined connection with these gurus....[85]

Some concerns about reductionism are valid. The question to ask is whether people lose any truth or value via reductionism. If so, then yes, one has gone too far. Dennett advises, "We must distinguish reductionism, which is in general a good thing, from *greedy reductionism*, which is not. The difference, in the context of Darwin's theory, is simple: greedy reductionists think that everything can be explained without cranes; good reductionists think that everything can be explained without skyhooks."[86]

Dennett's "cranes" and "skyhooks" are useful metaphors for describing tools with which to evolve designs faster, such that they look like they must have been created overnight or by some divine intelligence. The distinction is that cranes are powerful tools derived from evolution (e.g., a physical crane created by engineers to help with construction), the Baldwin Effect—a way for phenotypic learning to be passed on. In

---

84 "We'd like to thank you, Herbert Hoover/ For really showing us the way/ You dirty rat, you Bureaucrat, you/ Made us what we are today." From the musical *Annie*, these lyrics place the blame of the 1929 crash on Herbert Hoover.

85 Richard Geist, *Investor Therapy: A Psychologist and Investing Guru Tells You How to Out-Psych Wall Street* (New York: Crown Business, 2003).

86 Daniel C. Dennett, *Darwin's Dangerous Idea* (New York: Simon & Schuster Paperbacks, 1995).

the context of the trading, readily available market data, connectivity technology (e.g., FIX), and the plethora of good trading literature help traders leapfrog over numerous evolutionary steps to become more profitable traders faster.

Skyhooks, on the other hand, are the creations of miracles, angels, or advanced alien species. They are an "imaginary means of suspension from the sky."[87] Dennett surmises that a skyhook could be a concept from Greek drama, "when second-rate playwrights found their plots leading their heroes into inescapable difficulties, they were often tempted to crank down a god onto the scene, like Superman, to save the situation supernaturally."[88] People usually decry this sort of behavior by Hollywood writers, but somehow the bulk of the financial press is given free rein to assign sky-hooks galore.

The Fed, powerful governments, and hedge fund managers are all assigned praise and blame for the creation of all kinds of economic and market phenomena. Popular investment skyhooks include the genius of individual fund managers; secret, proprietary strategies; or technology and supernatural abilities to predict the future (and all its varieties). Interestingly, some system traders look for skyhooks as well. Ed Seykota and other famous traders have an almost cult-like following, and many system traders get caught searching for the holy grail (one super successful indicator or strategy).

Thus, good reductionists can see that all the complexity of investing can indeed be reduced to simplified strategies and executed mechanically, because they recognize all the hard work and effort of that goes into developing the building blocks and tools (cranes) of "simple strategies." System trading would be not be viable if investors did not have access to the quantity and quality of market data assembled diligently by vendors such as CSI, tickdata.com, and TradeStation.

System trading would be impossible without the modern computer, software programming languages, and the software programs that make both the coding and back-testing user-friendly. In other words, system trading may seem simple, but it utilizes very advanced technologies and, done right, can solve most of the valid issues critics bring up, e.g. adapting systems to overcome its static nature. In fact, system trading is far more sophisticated and technologically advanced than most fundamental, discretionary investing activities.

Looking for skyhooks, which is what many discretionary investors end up doing, is, at worst, irrational, and at best, messy. There is no integrated rational thought process taking place when looking for and assigning skyhooks to market phenomena. Betting on further Fed stimuli by buying stocks is a highly irrational investing activity, equivalent to what all skyhooking eventually leads to—gambling.

---

87 *Oxford English Dictionary.*
88 Daniel C. Dennett, *Darwin's Dangerous Idea* (New York: Simon & Schuster Paperbacks, 1995).

NATURAL INTELLIGENCE

Part of the anxiety with scientific methods in investing is a more specific discomfort with technology and engineering. It is perhaps best exemplified by the resistance toward artificial intelligence (AI) technologies. Before diving into AI, a clear, if broader, definition of technology would be useful. Technology is not just the GPS navigator in your car or the climate-controlled air-conditioner in your bedroom. Technology is more sophisticated computation. Computation of what? Information. A GPS computes geographical location, while air-conditioners compute temperature.

Given this broad definition of technology, one can see that technology is all around us—and has been for eons. All of nature employs basic strategies to compute information in a variety of ways; they may be singular strategies, but they are effective strategies nonetheless. Plants compute information about where to find water, sunlight, and oxygen. Ants compute information about where to find food and what roles to play. Markets compute information about price and value.

At the base of all technology lies engineering. Engineering is simply the application of knowledge to solve problems. It builds cranes to allow its users to manipulate and leverage information to their advantage (to optimize their objective functions). As Darwin defined evolution by natural selection as an algorithmic process, it follows that all of biological life is founded on engineering principles. Dennett is clear on this issue: "[T]he engineering perspective on biology is not merely occasionally useful, not merely a valuable option, but the obligatory organizer of all Darwinian thinking, and the primary source of its power."[89]

John von Neumann, who with Alan Turing is credited with inventing the modern computer, researched self-replicating programs in the 1950s. Far from the androids of science fiction lore, these automatons mimicked the behavior of cells and their intricate behavior of reproduction. That von Neumann was able to figure out the logic of cellular replication in repeatable form says much about the computational nature of life at its most fundamental level. As Dennett points out, Turing also did something similar in figuring out the algorithmic nature of how the complex shapes of organisms arise from a single cell.

Seen in this light, the term "artificial intelligence" is misleading. There is nothing artificial about the native intelligence found throughout nature. The algorithm of evolution is not artificial; it is very real and used throughout all of life on various levels to adapt and optimize. In this sense, all living things have some form of intelligence. Ants use a search algorithm that allows them to efficiently and effectively scavenge a forest floor clean in a surprisingly short period of time. Indeed, scientists, after ascertaining this algorithm, have been experimenting with applications of this technology for several years now.

89 Ibid.

After seeing the emergence of complex behavior from simple cellular automata, renowned scientist Stephen Wolfram proposed a "new law of nature" in his famous work, *A New Kind of Science*. The basic assumption of Wolfram's Principle of Computational Equivalence is that all basic processes in nature, whether thinking by a human brain or the development of weather systems, are forms of computation.

Throughout *A New Kind of Science,* Wolfram describes a variety of topics—from economics to quantum mechanics—in terms of computation, with simple rules. Each of these "computer programs" has strategies that can be are evolved by life forms throughout the universe. In fact, these strategies exist at all levels of life, everywhere.

Part of the reason investing is so hard that the market is so formless. More to the point, people are accustomed to master-slave, hierarchical organizations. This paradigm is the reason politicians and the media are always looking for a scapegoat; they think some specific person or group is controlling the markets. But like ants and most other interesting things in life, there is no one entity in control.

Rather, strategies and collections of strategies are always evolving by competing against and replicating parts or wholes of each other to form the organizations and designs in the market. Trading systems are the explicit manipulating and organization of these strategies for a trader's competitive advantage. It is both a contributor to and a result of the market processes.

By using AI technologies such as genetic algorithms and neural nets, a system trader can greatly enhance the competitive effectiveness of his or her strategies in the market. AI technologies are among the most effective cranes available, because they allow for a more systematic and efficient search of useable strategies latent within the market. As such, system trading in its most genuine form is a highly evolved, efficient method of solving problems.

SYSTEM TRADING (DEVELOPMENT) AS SEARCH HEURISTIC

> "Scientific discovery can be viewed as a parameter search in a large and extremely inhomogeneous space."

—Joseph Phillips[90]

Mainstream thought often focuses on finding the one "right" answer—the one right way to invest, the one right way to run a country. Of course, most of the important and interesting aspects of life do not have one "right" answer. In fact, there are usually several different "right" answers, of varying degrees of "rightness." A great deal of scientific

90 Joseph Phillips, "Towards a Method of Searching a Diverse Theory Space for Scientific Discovery" (DS '01 Proceedings of the 4th International Conference on Discovery Science, 2001).

progress is made by searching for a "better," "more optimal" solution to a well-specified problem.

A search heuristic is a general method of finding a solution to a problem in a large set of possible solutions. But life in general is in a continual process of searching for newer and better solutions to sets of problems. Throughout the natural world, the search heuristic most responsible for solving its many problems is evolution itself. As Beinhocker writes, "evolution is a general-purpose and highly powerful recipe for finding innovative solutions to complex problems. It is a learning algorithm that adapts to changing environments and accumulates knowledge over time."[91]

Daniel Dennett introduced this view of evolution as an algorithm in *Darwin's Dangerous Idea,* the ideas of which undergird most of the interesting things happening in science and culture at large today. What Phillips is alluding to is that many of the ideas and solutions are already there, waiting to be put together by the building blocks already in existence. As the ultimate search heuristic, evolution is very extremely effective in searching through the large, "inhomogenous" space of possible solutions.

Dennett defines it crisply: "The theoretical power of Darwin's abstract scheme was due to several features that Darwin quite firmly identified...but lacked the terminology to describe explicitly. Today we could capture these features under a single term. Darwin had discovered the power of an *algorithm*."[92] Dennett further elucidates:

> Here, then, is Darwin's dangerous idea: the algorithmic level *is* the level that best accounts for the speed of the antelope, the wing of the eagle, the shape of the orchid, the diversity of species, and all the other occasions for wonder in the world of nature. It is hard to believe that something as mindless and mechanical as an algorithm could produce such wonderful things. No matter how impressive the products of an algorithm, the underlying process always consists of nothing but a set of individually mindless steps succeeding each other without the help of any intelligent supervision....[93]

What evolution is particularly good at is automatically creating what Dennett calls "Good Tricks for survival." If survival is the problem, these "tricks" are the solutions that the search heuristic of evolution finds. What's amazing about evolution is that solutions can be derived from very simple building blocks. Beinhocker's discussion of LEGO sets is a great example:

---

91 Eric Beinhocker, *The Origin of Wealth* (Boston: Harvard Business School Press, 2006).
92 Daniel C. Dennett, *Darwin's Dangerous Idea* (New York: Simon & Schuster Paperbacks, 1995).
93 Ibid.

Even the simplest blocks can be attached in a large number of permutations; for example, two of the little rectangular blocks that are one dimple wide by two dimples long…can be put together in fourteen distinct permutations of attachment positions…and two 2-by-2 blocks can be attached in thirty-three ways. As the number of blocks, their size and the number of attachment options grow, the number of possible permutations explodes. The total number of possible structures that can be constructed from even a modest-sized LEGO set is mind-bogglingly enormous….Nonetheless, the number is finite. Evolutionary theorists call such a set of possible permutations a *design space*….But buried somewhere deep in the heart of the library (of possible LEGO designs) is a fabulous 384-block design for a LEGO spaceship…a fascinating 220-block LEGO horse, as well as a 405-block LEGO castle….But despite the trillions of variants on castle designs, such "interesting" designs are exceedingly rare….There are far, far more boring, random, gibberish designs.[94]

Thus, combinations of small buildings blocks become the solutions to life's problems. Effective search heuristics are great at going through these combinations to find an optimal solution. Thus, the building blocks for an TV advertisement can be sounds, colors, images, and words. These building blocks can be combined in any number of ways to entice us to buy products.

Many of the standard technical indicators traders use today were created by J. Welles Wilder in his seminal work, *New Concepts in Technical Trading Systems* (Hunter Publishing Company, 1978). In this book, Wilder invented the RSI, Parabolic, ADX, and SAR (stop and reversal) methods of trading. In his introduction, Wilder discusses the various tools necessary to calculate these indicators, such as the HP-41CV calculator. The indicators themselves are built on simple mathematical concepts. The book is an interesting read, as Wilder walks through the calculation of each indicator step-by-step. Though taken for granted now, these indicators founded the technical analysis domain and represented the cutting edge in trading at that time.

In the pursuit of greater profit and lower cost of time and energy (more efficient analysis of markets), Wilder's unique talents allowed him to construct something novel from existing building blocks, providing a solution that greatly increased the fitness or effectiveness of trading capabilities. TradeStation's easy language, Ward Systems' easy-to-use AI software products, automated trading platforms, and the Globex have all contributed to increased trading capabilities to varying degrees.

Looking at any type of creative activity, such as scientific discovery or new product development, as a simple act of problem solving has the sting of reductionism to it, but all of what people see around them is the result of such solutions. Necessity, competi-

---

94   Eric Beinhocker, *The Origin of Wealth* (Boston: Harvard Business School Press, 2006).

tion, and boredom are all powerful forces of invention and can all be seen as attempts to solve problems: to fill a hole, to become better, to do something new.

PROBLEM SOLVING OR SOLUTION SEARCHING

Even complicated activities such as scientific inquiry and discovery can be seen as a problem-solving activity; by doing so, scientists have been able to create automated systems that replicate what human scientists can do. These are called *expert systems*. The first was DENDRAL, short for Dendritic Algorithm. Its goal was to be able to discover the topological structure of organic compounds through the use of indirect observations.

To solve this problem, scientists needed to be able to ascertain not only the compound's constituent atoms but also the arrangement of these atoms. By being fed knowledge of chemistry and other pertinent data (its mass spectra), DENDRAL was able to generate numbers of possible solutions by the same type of combinatorics employed by many heuristics. Then, by narrowing down the solution set, DENDRAL was able to generate solutions (correct answers about the structure) that rivaled the performance of expert scientists.

How are solutions actually found in this manner? It helps to expand the perception of what constitutes a problem. Going back the ant colony, consider foraging for food in a forest. The problem would be sustenance. The solution would be food that is edible, tasty, or healthy. The forest would be the search or solution space. Ants have developed their own search algorithm to solve this problem; with it, they are able to scour a large geographical area and locate food in an efficient manner. This algorithm is so successful that a class of ant colony optimization algorithms are used by scientists now.

The forest floor is a physical representation of what scientists refer to as a *search space*. It is generally represented by a 3D graph, with the *x*- and *y*-axes representing the parameters of the system and located on the horizontal plane. The *z*-axis, or the vertical axis, represents the score of each combination of *x* and *y* values. This score is the fitness value, or score, that is being optimized by the search algorithm. The solution with the highest score is the best solution available in that search space.

Because the forest floor is an actual geographical location, *x* and *y* would represent map coordinates, with *z* representing the amount of food. If an engineer is designing a simple robot and trying to figure out the design that would make it go fastest, *x* could represent the length of the legs, and *y* could represent the weight of the robot. *Z* would obviously represent speed.

Thus, running a combinatorics search through all the different combinations of leg length and weight of the robot and then calculating its speed would allow the engineer to find the best combination of long legs and low weight. A statistics program could compute such a search and then graphically display all the values in a 3D graph. The engineer would see a surface graph, the topology of which might show interesting relationships between the different sets.

As shown in Graph 1 below, there is an optimal value, and the parameters nearby have a slightly lower score. Many search spaces look like this graph, with one peak and the remaining values sloping down as its score gets lower and lower. But this smooth decline from a single peak is an idealization; real-world search spaces are rough, with sharp peaks, surrounded by cliffs that abruptly drop off. These systems are brittle and have one random solution that may just mean it was a lucky search. An example is shown in Graph 2 below.

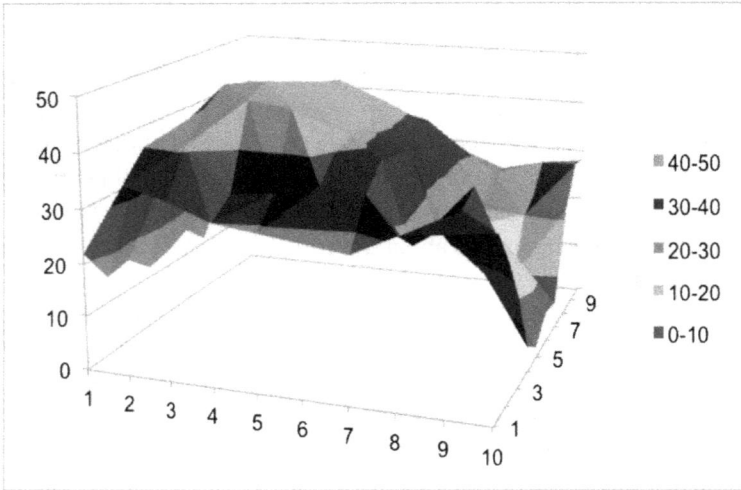

Graph 1

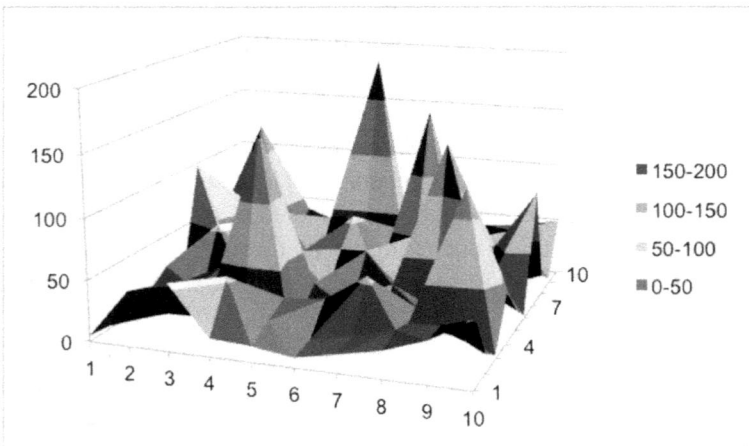

Graph 2

Search spaces are also called *fitness landscapes,* because the candidate solutions are spaced and ordered based on their fitness values. The geographical lingo helps in locating or identifying features of the data. More generally, a fitness landscape can contain entire strategies or systems, each one representing a candidate solution, such as one book from the Dennett's library or one collection of genes. Larger search spaces have small hills scattered about, big mountains with long ranges, vast empty spaces (representing no solutions in those parameter sets), jagged edges, cliffs, valleys, and rounded tops. In these search spaces lie the solutions to life's biggest problems—the best DNA, the best car design, the best-selling fashion line, or the best investment strategy. Each of these solutions has a fitness score, and together they create the fitness landscape.

For investing, the problem is how to make money in the markets in a safe way. Said another way, a trader is looking for a solution with a high Calmar or Sharpe ratio in an infinite solution set, or possible trading strategies. In an infinitely large "best investment strategy" landscape, where the fitness value would be one metric combining net return and the Calmar ratio, and each candidate solution would represent some combination of rules, indicators, filters, and anything else related to the markets, one would likely see vast deserts sprinkled lightly with small mounds and a few relatively large hills. One strategy would be to buy at three o'clock. One would include all the standard technical indicators found in the standard charting software. The hills would represent the best strategies, comprised of some successful combination of rules.

The good news is that there is an infinite number of novel systems to be developed. There are those systems that a given investor has not found yet that other have, and there are those that are completely novel. A static landscape would be difficult to address, but the reality is that this landscape is constantly changing. Hence, trying to find these exploitable strategies latent in the market with ad hoc testing and experimenting becomes a costly chore. Why not copy ant colonies or DNA—the natural intelligence discussed above—a la DENDRAL? That is, why not let the computer search this space of indicators in a more thorough, efficient manner, using AI technologies?

ARTIFICIAL INTELLIGENCE

Search heuristics as a field has grown rapidly over the past few decades. Currently, genetic algorithms, genetic programming, and evolutionary strategies are some of the most widely used. Many other search heuristics mimic biological systems, such as swarm-based (particle swarm and ant colony optimization) systems. The first three mentioned above are specific technologies based on the more general evolutionary algorithm. Evolution, it turns out, is arguably the greatest of all search heuristics. Its effectiveness in shaping a fitness landscape is unmatched in its efficiency and effectiveness.

Paraphrasing Beinhocker's excellent discussion of fitness landscapes in *The Origin of Wealth*, there are two key features of natural, real-world fitness landscapes. The first is that evolution cannot look ahead. It sounds obvious, but for a solution seeker, nothing is more stifling. The fact is, some fitness landscapes do not have any hills or mountains; that is, there are no solutions. A researcher or developer could spend his or her entire life searching one corner of the landscape and not find anything. There are no guarantees that intelligence, skills, and effort will pay off.

Second, the search space is constantly changing. As mentioned above, even if the landscape stayed the same, the sheer size of the space makes it incredibly difficult to navigate it. But a changing landscape adds an entirely new level of difficulty. Solutions found today are gone tomorrow. New solutions are found in areas once thought barren. If the reader has ever wondered why true innovations are so rare, this is the reason.

But there is hope; after all, ants have figured out an effective way. That is, searching for food on the forest floor would be much easier if the landscape and the food stayed put. But they do not. Trees fall, ants carry away food, food rots, winds move objects around. In a constantly changing landscape, flexibility or adaptability becomes critical. One has to be able to move around in a systematic fashion to quickly find sufficient sources of food.

In such a search space, Beinhocker notes that two different types of search strategies are effective, although they exhibit notable limitations. An *adaptive walk* tries out a solution by trying a new combination closest to it. On the fitness landscape, it takes one step in a random direction; if it is better than the current solution, it will use that as the default choice. If not, it will try another solution in a different direction. In an actual search, the parameters limit the choices such that at any one decision point, there are a limited number of choices available. An adaptive walk will "walk" up the fitness scale by searching thus, finding better and better solutions.

The problem is that in a large search space, it must start somewhere. As it walks up the fitness scale by finding the best or optimal solution in the vicinity where it first started, it gets stranded there on top of its hill (these heuristics are called "hill-climbing" techniques). The only way it can find another, better solution is to walk down that hill, but there is no mechanism for doing so. This limitation can easily translate into opportunity risk: "The adaptive walk could even get stuck on a molehill right in the middle of a field of Everests."[95]. This hill is called a local maximum as opposed to a global maximum, which would be the theoretical best solution of all.

In effect, what is happening is that the adaptive walk is taking a limited number of parts to construct a solution that works very well in a small, restricted environment. Consider a trader who starts his or her career trading the S&P during its volatile early days. Using a volatility breakout system, the trader is so successful with it that he or she develops better and better versions of it. However, by not trying other markets and other strategies, the trader severely limits his or her trading performance. In this example, the fitness scale would be net profits, which would be limited by the trader's singular approach to trading. The trader is stuck on the S&P hill and cannot get off. The trading

---

95 Ibid.

of trend-following strategies on the Euro, crude oil, and copper become significant opportunities—other hills on the search space of trading strategies—the trader misses out on; the opportunity cost becomes enormous. Worse, if the landscape made up of the S&P market changes, the trader's volatility breakout system becomes a loser, and he or she ends up crashing down into a valley of poor performance.

The second strategy, which Beinhocker calls a *random jump*, allows for random jumps across the entire landscape. No longer restricted to its nearest neighbor, a search can climb a hill and then jump clear across to another hill; thus it is better able to find a global maximum. The random jump is far more flexible; hence, it would not get stuck and crash if the landscape were to change—it could simply jump to a new area and look for new solutions. So the payout with this strategy can be huge. However, there are far more valleys and flat areas on a landscape, and the chance on jumping on to another hill is quite small. More likely, the search will end up in a valley. Just by the natural construction of landscapes, "there will always be many more ways to make yourself worse off than better off."[96]

If one had to choose between these two strategies, one would be stuck between choosing a low-risk, low-reward strategy and a high-risk, high-reward strategy. Well, can a combination of the two work? Yes, it can. Evolution is just such a heuristic. It combines these two algorithms and allows for "an adaptive walk to keep us climbing higher and higher in the landscape, but also gives us a few random jumps to keep us from getting stuck on local peaks."[97]

Further, as Beinhocker points out, evolution does more: it can weight random jumps toward smaller ones, so that the riskier, longer jumps have a lower probability of occurring. Further, instead of just one search activity or hill-climbing taking place, evolution generates multiple searches simultaneously, constantly climbing and jumping around the landscape for the best solutions (think of Hofstadter's parallel terraced scan).

This last feature is significant. With multiple solutions searching the landscape, many of them would end up grouped together around local maxima. They would all climb up, and once they reach the top, they would start to spread out. But then a few solutions would make a random jumps across the landscape and find other local maxima, some smaller, but some greater. Some of them would jump into a valley, search randomly around, and then find a hill to climb that could lead to the best solution thus far, continually leading to better and better solutions.

It is amazing to watch vibrant economies, such as the US economy, continually come up with novel industries. Just when it seemed the Internet had reached a plateau, social networking came along and engendered a new industry with combinations of old, new, and entirely different technologies and paradigms. These innovations and successes can come about because, thus far, the United States has been able to maintain enough freedom and diversity to allow for random jumps into new areas.

---

96 Ibid.
97 Ibid.

In countries with less dynamic economies, such as the Republic of Korea (South Korea), governmental and societal forces often conspire to prevent such jumps. Students are pushed toward conventional academic paths (doctor, government official); students wanting to develop software, become a rock star, study Swahili, or become the next UFC champion are strongly discouraged.

Many new business models, such as hedge funds, are discouraged by strict regulations that protect incumbents. The communal culture of Korean financial firms discourages outliers, the very individuals who can make those jumps to new sources of revenue. Thus, Korea has fewer "jumpers." The consequence is that Korea has far fewer local maxima on different areas of the economic revenue landscape than countries such as the United States and is also more at risk to falter when the larger landscape of the global economy changes.

Hopefully this situation will change. Evolution's natural path is to allow for the spreading of interactors to find all the novel, wonderful solutions out there. This type of diverse search is critical to the continuity of a society and to generating innovation.

> This kind of spreading of bets across a population is exactly what evolution does-each interactor (or in biology, organism) can be considered a hiker. The process of replication powers the adaptive walk. If high-fitness hikers tend to recombine their schemata with other high-fitness hikers and have more offspring then low-fitness hikers, then the cloud of hikers tends to grow at higher altitudes and shrink at lower ones. But the process of differentiation (in biology, through crossover and mutation) ensures that we have hikers spread out across the landscape. Most will be bunched relatively close together in the same region-this is a good thing because if the hikers are alive at all, they know that they are at least somewhere above the poison fog of selection and, as noted, there are always more ways down than up. However, there will also be at least a few outliers providing a chance of finding some new ways to higher ground.[98]

For these reasons, among the many varieties of search heuristics, evolutionary approaches have been the most influential and most widely used. Genetic algorithms (GA) feature both the adaptive walk and random jump strategies to effectively find optimal solutions. The utility of using GA in trading is the ability to search the infinitely large "best investment strategy" landscape in a more comprehensive, yet efficient way. This latter point is important to anyone developing systems, as searching through all the combinations of a small number of indicators and their parameter values would take warehouses of servers tens of thousands of years to backtest. GAs can search these spaces much faster, and this speed is the primary motivation behind their use in parameter optimizations.

---

98 Ibid.

The problem GA solves for traders is how to modify trading systems to changing market conditions. A volatility-breakout system with a static parameter set employed while crude oil is trading at $20 would likely have gone bust over the past five years, simply because the average daily range has quintupled. But extend this line of thinking a bit further. What happens if volatility suddenly contracts, as it did in 2009 after the volatility explosion of 2008? All volatility-breakout systems, which are long volatility strategies, will do poorly. The cause is not the parameters, but the entry rules.

In such rapidly changing markets, the best solution is to be able to create adaptive trading systems that can, following the rigors of science, find the best solutions for a new market environment. So, ideally, this adaptive trading method would shut down the volatility-breakout strategies in early 2009, as data becomes available telling it that volatility is shrinking and to search through other combinations of strategies to evolve a better strategy (e.g., countertrend system). This adaptability is about as close to a real-life holy grail as there is, but GAs can make this a reality (albeit only with a great deal of skill and experience).

So what exactly are GAs? In the next section, they will be examined in detail as a prologue to the adaptive trading system discussed at the end of the book. In sum, system trading in its essence is the search for patterns; it is the evolutionary activity of searching the solution or strategy space for strategies. It is this aspect that makes system trading a far more *natural* way of investing in the markets.

INTRODUCTION TO GENETIC ALGORITHMS (GA)

A GA is basically evolution boiled down to its simplest parts. Using inheritance, mutation, natural selection, and crossover, GAs are a class of powerful search heuristics used in many real-world applications. The traveling salesman problem is a well-known sample problem used to test and compare search heuristics. GAs are well-suited to this type of problem and are used in warehouse management, logistics, transportation, telecommunications, and manufacturing processes. GAs are also used extensively throughout the sciences, most especially in clinical diagnosis and the biological sciences. Their real power lies in finding adaptive solutions in changing environments.

GA use in the financial sector has been limited to some hedge funds as well as institutional trading departments, and a healthy number of papers have also been published by the academic community regarding financial applications of GA. Chaoshunter, by Ward Systems (www.wardsystems.com), is a user-friendly, yet powerful software package specifically designed for trading system development that uses a GA. Mike Barna of Trading System Lab (www.tradingsystemlab.com) has developed a full trading system development software program. The program uses genetic programming, which is a proprietary technology based on genetic algorithms, but uses a more flexible and powerful representation scheme.[99]

GA's representation borrows from the structure and processes of DNA, hence the name. Candidate solutions are represented as strings of binary bits (groups of numbers so they can be easily manipulated), for example, 1101010001. These are often called *chromosomes,* and this structure allows for complicated candidate solutions to be represented and manipulated. Parts of the strings or groups of bits can be deleted, which would mean a specific trait is being killed off, or switched with the bits of another string, which represents traits being replaced or reproduced. Bits in a chromosome can also be randomly changed, which would represent mutation.

In her book, Mitchell provides an excellent, accessible discussion of a genetic algorithm. The entire algorithm or recipe is simple enough:

1) Generate an initial population of candidate solutions. Candidate solutions can be strategies, programs, systems, or rule sets that mimic biological organisms.

   a) Each candidate is represented by a string of bits.

   b) The bits represent the parts of the candidate that can be mated with others and changed (mutated) randomly.

2) Calculate the fitness of each candidate.

3) Select the best candidates to become the parents of the next generation.

4) Generate next generation of candidates.

   a) Pair parents together by recombining parts (reproduction of good traits).

   b) Generate random mutations of the parents (introduction of novelty).

   c) Parents continue mating with each other (maximize number of combinations) until equal to initial population.

5) Go back to step 2.

Mitchell then provides a fun, interesting example of her GA at work. Robby is her robot that is charged with picking up soda cans littered throughout his world (similar to ants foraging for food). How would a programmer instruct Robby to pick up these cans? Mitchell's own program is basically as follows: "If there is a can in the current site, pick it up. Otherwise, if there is a can in one of the adjacent sites, move to that site. Otherwise, choose a random direction to move in." Testing her simple strat-

---

99 Genetic Programming is another popular evolution-based search heuristic developed by John R. Koza. It is designed to evolve computer programs, and its representation scheme consists of syntax trees, most often expressed in LISP.

egy on 10,000 cleaning sessions (simulation runs), her strategy scored a 346 on a possible 500.

She then constructs a GA to allow Robby to evolve his own strategy. First, she generates an initial population of 200 random strategies. Here, a strategy takes form: if Robby is in a certain situation A, then he will do action B. So each strategy is made up of two parts—Robby's situation and its corresponding instruction.

Mitchell comes up with 243 different possible situations with the variables "empty," "contains a can," or "wall" in each of the five spots (current, north, south, east west). So Robby looks at each of the five spots and ascertains whether it is empty, contains a can, or is a wall, and then takes one of seven different actions (the instructions): MoveNorth, MoveSouth, MoveEast, MoveWest, StayPut, PickUp, and RandomMove.

A strategy is a long list of all the actions that each of the 243 situations calls for. So when Robby finds himself in a new spot, he looks to his strategy and finds that if he is in this particular spot (e.g., North=Empty, South=Empty, East=Empty, West=Empty, Current=Empty), then his action should be to MoveNorth. Another strategy would instruct Robby to MoveWest in the same situation. And strategy 3 would instruct Robby to PickUp in the same situation. So these strategies will be evolved by the GA to give Robby the best instructions given a certain situation.

To code these strategies so they can be evolved by the GA software program, situations are designated by position, and instructions are designated by a number from 0 to 6: 0=MoveNorth, 1=MoveSouth, 2=MoveEast, 3=MoveWest, 4=StayPut, 5=PickUp, and 6=RandomMove. Here is what a sample strategy, strategy 1, looks like:

```
23300323421630343530546006102562515114162260435654334066511514
15650220647064205100664321616152165202236443336334601332650300
40622050243165006111305146664232401254633455241264324413610202
150630642551654043264463156164510543665346310551164600516
```

The first position is the situation North=Empty, South=Empty, East=Empty, West=Empty, Current=Empty. The number 2 in that position means that Robby will MoveEast. Thus, the situations represented by each position are fixed for every strategy in this GA scheme; only the instructions vary.

Going back to GA parlance, then, the strategy is represented as a chromosome (the long string of numbers above). The instruction or action is the gene, which is represented as a bit or number. Each chromosome is a list or combination of genes, and these chromosomes are then subjected to the crossover and mutation functions to evolve the best, most optimal strategy.

Specifically, each strategy is selected based on its fitness score, which measures how well Robby picks up the cans. Then the strategies are evolved in three ways. First, parents are chosen probabilistically based on their score; that is, the better their scores are, the better their chance of being chosen. Second, the genes of each chromosome are crossed over (the parents are mated) by randomly choosing one place to split the binary sequence and then switching the halves. Third, mutation occurs by randomly changing numbers in the chromosomes (e.g., a 0 turns into a 6).

So what were the results? Mitchell took the best strategy after 1,000 generations and then ran it on 10,000 cleaning sessions (new and different than the ones that "trained" the systems, i.e., out-of-sample), and the average score was 483 out of 500. Once the strategy is taken apart and played out in detail,[100] one can see some amazing strategies that GA "stumbled" upon that demonstrate the intelligence of the program. The significant advantage is that the GA strategy can be run on any can-filled space and realistic can-filled spaces that constantly change. The same GA program would be able to find the optimal strategy for every space. This adaptability is GA's biggest strength.

BEAGLE'S (FORSYTH) SCHEME (HERB)

This advantage was demonstrated more clearly in a study conducted by Richard Forsyth. Richard Forsyth's BEAGLE was one of the first programs offering GA capability. In his paper,[101] he provides an example of the effectiveness of his algorithm with a case study comparison between a Statistical Package for the Social Sciences (SPSS) and BEAGLE. SPSS is a statistical analysis software program that can help physicians with decision-making tasks, especially in diagnosis of patient data. This study is interesting, because the superiority of statistical reasoning in clinical diagnosis has already been demonstrated (see cognitive bias chapter). Genetic algorithms seem to take this progression a step further in the right direction.

Based on certain patient diagnosis variables, such as mean arterial pressure and red cell index, SPSS was able to classify correctly 75 percent of the cases (i.e., between those cases in which the patient survived and those which the patient died). BEAGLE had a success rate of 81 percent. This specific rule was found after 500 generations and was significantly simpler than the functions used in the SPSS. Other studies have been done supporting the effectiveness of GAs in clinical diagnosis.[102]

BEAGLE's algorithm is constructed in the following way. Fitness values are calculated thus: ((goodness-minscore)*100*gfactor)/(maxscore-minscore)-size. "goodness" is the fitness function, and "size" is the length or size of the rule. Thus, long rules are penalized. "gfactor" can be set to alter the balance between goodness and size, with a low setting selecting shorter rules. In practice, GAs can generate optimal solutions that are too long and impractical to implement.

The procedure is as follows:

---

100 Mitchell walks through this GA-generated, winning strategy in illuminating detail (pp. 136–40)

101 Richard Forsyth, "BEAGLE—A Darwinian Approach to Pattern Recognition," *Kybernetes* (1981).

102 Two notable examples include "Comparison of Genetic Algorithms and Other Classification Methods in the Diagnosis of Female Urinary Incontinence," J. Laurikkala, M. Julhola, S. Lammi, and K. Viikki (1999); and "Classification of Breast Cancer Using Genetic Algorithms and Tissue Microarrays," Marisa Dolled-Filhart, Lisa Rydén, Melissa Cregger, Karin Jirström, Malini Harigopal, Robert L. Camp, and David L. Rimm (2006).

1) The top 25 percent are left alone.

2) The second quarter is subjected to a program called GROW, which adds a node to the string. This node is chosen randomly. GROW is the first random mutation component of the algorithm. GROW is reproductive and tries to improve potentially good nodes.

3) The third quarter is subjected to SLIM, which takes away a node from the string. This node is also chosen randomly. SLIM is the second random mutation component of the algorithm. SLIM is the obverse of GROW and is trying to eliminate bad nodes from the gene pool.

4) The bottom 25 percent are killed off completely.

5) To replace this bottom 25 percent, rules from the top 50 percent are mated. A subtree from one parent is randomly chosen and combined with another. The operator connecting the two subtrees is also chosen randomly; this MATE procedure results in a new rule.

6) A MUTATION procedure is subjected to a few, randomly selected rules/strategies in the lower 7/8ths. MUTATION can change operators, swap subtrees, etc.

The GROW, SLIM, MATE, and MUTATION procedures produce a new generation of rules/strategies, which are then run through the same training data set.

GAs provide a systematic and elegant way to find the most optimal parameters and rules of investment strategies. Optimal solutions found with GAs are different from the results found through the "optimization" available on trading packages. These optimization programs are really combinatoric functions without the adaptive functionality of a GA. A common parameter optimization search typically involves a trader setting the range within which the program basically looks to find the best combination.

The drawback with this approach is that the trader will get stuck on a local maximum defined by the initial parameter value range he or she inputted. GAs are mutation operators that introduce novelty to kick the search off the local maximum; thus, they can find a novel parameter that works best in a new market environment. The other advantage is that by mating two strategies, there is a chance that a good part of a bad strategy can be used elsewhere, where it may improve the results.

This flexibility and novelty is why GA is categorized as nonlinear. In an optimization procedure, each candidate or possible solution is a single point in the search space. A deterministic optimization method can only explore a linear set of points, whereas a GA explores multiple points in a multidimensional search space. Hence, with GAs, system traders can scientifically, systematically, and rationally trade the market with the utmost flexibility and adaptability.

SUMMARY

System trading is the scientific and systematic application of market price analysis. Its goal is to optimize risk-adjusted returns; to this end, it allows for the application of a wide range of powerful tools. To many, system trading's mechanical nature is its greatest weakness. This chapter has tried to show that this feature is in fact its greatest strength.

The criticisms of its mechanical nature demonstrate the deep misunderstanding investors have about the engineering of natural intelligence fundamental to all living things. Processing information, constructing designs, evolving, and adapting those designs is the domain of evolution. Indeed, as Wolfram demonstrated, all basic processes in nature are forms of computation. System trading is simply one specific application of these principles.

Due to its quantitative nature, system trading is essence is a method for efficiently finding profitable strategies, using the very processes that have shaped our world.

Nature has shown itself to be highly effective in finding solutions to problems. Through the mindless, mechanical process of evolution, everything from genes to ants can forage through search spaces to find optimal sources of food and fitter gene combinations. *System trading makes explicit and scientific what many investors are implicitly trying to do every day: find better strategies to profit from markets.*

Moreover, as seen with GAs, system trading may be mechanical, but it is by no means the static, inflexible method characterized by its critics. Rather, through the application of AI, system trading can adapt to changing market conditions in a scientifically valid way.

THE RATIONALITY OF SYSTEM TRADING

To review, a rational method of investing must include the following four requirements:

1) Testable: all necessary and sufficient rules within the system are clearly defined and integrated coherently
2) Clear objective
3) Evidence of efficacy: evidence that it is profitable (meets its objective/utility maximization)
4) Logical validity: methods core components must be logical valid

TESTABLE

Because systems must be coded to be tested, all backtested systems are in falsifiable form. In fact, as with all software programs, unless the ideas are explicitly laid out, systems will not be accepted for testing by backtesting programs. Because all knowledge is only provisionally true, a system can be continually tested with new data in an attempt to falsify it. Falsified systems can then be improved upon or scrapped, thereby preventing unnecessary losses.

CLEAR OBJECTIVE

Along with its rules, a system's objective function must also be specified before a back-testing program can start the test. Most system traders develop their systems to maximize not profits, but some risk-adjusted measure of profit, such as the Sharpe Ratio or the Calmar Ratio. Indeed, any optimization or evolutionary process cannot start without some quantifiable objective to maximize.

EVIDENCE OF EFFICACY

System trading provides a clear way to demonstrate that a given strategy does indeed generate profits before one starts to trade. Properly conducted, a backtest will demonstrate the profitability of the trading system. Backtesting is based on statistics, whose superiority over intuitive reasoning was discussed in chapter 5. Meehl's work clearly demonstrates that in uncertain and complex situations, simple human judgment is highly inadequate for calculating the necessary variables to generate an accurate probability assessment.

Meehl's work also highlights another reason for the superiority of systematic, statistical reasoning over intuitive judgment: humans have a hard time making decisions the same way for every situation. That is, if confronted with a topping market, an investor's judgment will call for a variety of reactions instead of executing the same response consistently. Without this consistency, it is difficult to generate the positive expectancy latent in a strategy over the long term.

LOGICAL VALIDITY

From the start, system trading begins with a sound rational foundation. Prospect theory (PT) demonstrated the significant difference between the way people *should* think and the way they *actually* think. The normative model PT was contrasted with was the Expected Value Model (EVM). System traders use a version of this model in evaluating possible trading systems, called *positive expectancy* (PE). Conformity to this model is one of the key reasons system trading can be counted on to produce rational strategies for investing.

Backtesting always starts with suspicion. Specifically, it assumes that any positive performance from a backtest is due to good luck or because it was overfit to the historical data. When the backtest provides evidence to the contrary, the trader has a logical basis for expecting profits in the future from this system. However, backtesting does not offer certainty. A correctly preformed backtest gives the trader evidence contrary to his null hypothesis that his system's profitability is due to chance. Evidence that negates this null hypothesis gives the trader enough "proof" to expect future profits from the system. The key point is that using a valid form of reasoning in this manner provides a rational way to invest.

There are different ways to express the null hypothesis in system trading. Typically, a trader will use statistical significance to void the null hypothesis that any profits his system generates are due to sheer chance. Another way is to formulate the null hypothesis such that any profits generated in the backtest are due to overfitting to historical data and, hence, the system will not be profitable in the future. Then, cross-validation or walk-forward analysis can be used to reject the null hypothesis—that is, if consistent profits are generated by walk-forward testing, one would conclude that the profits are *not* due to overfitting.

CHAPTER 7. KEY TOPICS IN SYSTEM TRADING

CURVE-FITTING

Backtesting is a specific version of predictive modeling. One way to characterize predictive modeling is to see it as an exercise in fitting a line (a.k.a. curve) to a bunch of data points.

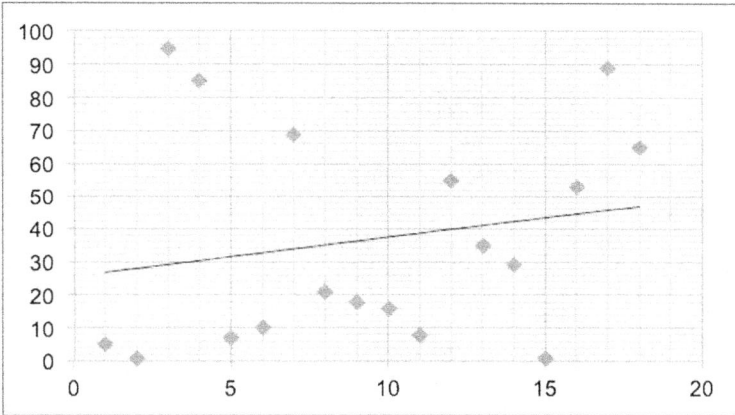

The line is called the curve, and it does
not fit the data points very well in this example.

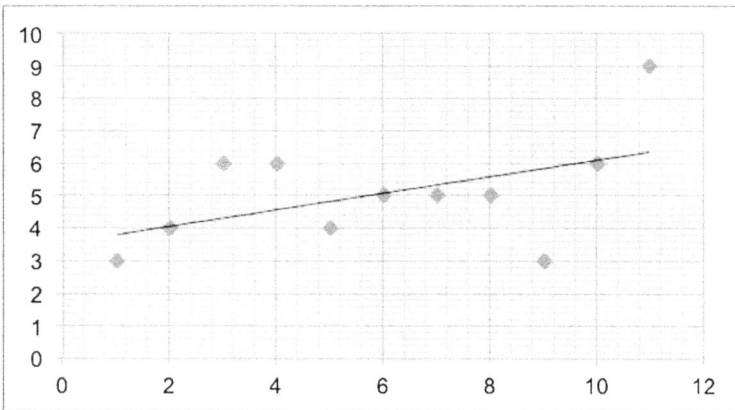

This curve fits the data points much better.

Predictive modeling typically starts with a set of data. These data are plotted on a graph, where the data points are the product of some formula with two or more variables—say, *x* and *y*. If the data form a generalized pattern—say, steadily going up from left to right—this pattern would represent graphically the relationship between the two variables, thereby allowing one to form conclusions about the model.

This pattern is generalized by drawing, say a simple, straight line amidst those steadily rising data points that captures the most number of data points. That line represents the formula that models the relationship between the two variables. This line or curve can take many forms. A straight line going up at a 45-degree angle is the most recognizable and basically says that if *x* increases by one unit, *y* also increases by one unit. The curve can go up, down, sideways, or curve all around in an attempt to best "fit" itself to the various data points.

Why draw a curve in the first place? Because by extending that curve further along, one can predict subsequent points. Extend the curve further to the right, where no data points yet exist, and the model is predicting where the next data points will occur in the future.

This type of modeling is called *linear regression*, and it is the basic activity of statistical modeling and prediction. Look at diagram 4 <diagrams 2, 3 are down and straight>. The data points here are varied, but they do cluster around certain points. A straight line with two variables cannot capture the relationships here. Indeed, these data points were created with five variables.

To build a model that mathematically describes the relationship between all five variables, multiple regression (more than two variables) must be employed. With multiple regression, one can create a curve that twists and turns around the data points. The more variables in the formula, the more twists and turns one can create. The more twists and turns the curve has, the more data points it can touch, and the more optimized it has become to that data set.

Taken to an extreme, one could literally try to fit every single data point, as shown in diagram 5. But consider the problem here. Try to extend the curve into the future to predict the next data point, and there is no rationally justified answer. In other words, the more optimized a curve becomes, the less predictive power it has. This problem, in essence, is overfitting. *Hence, one can characterize all of backtesting as curve-fitting. The system is the model that is being optimized to the historical data set. The trader is trying to find a curve (the trading system) that can best fit the data points and can also be extended into the future to capture future data points. The problem comes when the trader fits his or her model with too many variables and draws a curve that is far too twisty.*

OVERFITTING (OF)

Although it is encountered in many fields of research, scientists have yet to define exactly what OF is. One characteristic of OF that everyone agrees on is the significant discrepancy between tested and actual results (i.e., a backtest says the system is a winner, but in real time the system causes significant losses).

Another way to think about it is to see what happens if one were to delete or change a few of the data points. A straight curve would not be affected much if a few of the data points were taken away. However, an OF line would look very different if a few data points anywhere were deleted. This "sensitivity" or "brittleness" is the mark of OF. The goal is to develop robust trading systems.

In effect, the curve has memorized past data too well. However, that is not what a predictive model should do. Instead of learning, the curve has simply memorized information. Instead of generalizing and finding a pattern of behavior that can persist, it has picked specific points for which no larger pattern exists.

DEGREES OF FREEDOM (DF)

Referring back to the example in diagram 5 one can see why using more data may not necessarily prevent OF. One can still construct a curve that fits a large data set and is so twisty that it cannot successfully predict the next data point. In other words, OF is not simply due to too small a sample data set; it is also due to the degree of the model's complexity. Hence, one good solution is to keep the number of parameters in a trading system low relative to the amount of data on which it is tested. In statistical terms, this practice works because it preserves DF.

OF occurs most frequently when too many constraints are placed on the test data. Instead of allowing for the randomness latent in the data, the system constricts the randomness out. Mathematically, this constriction is measured with DF. DF is the measure of dependence on the rules and the rules' specific parameter values: the more rules and the greater the parameter optimization, the heavier the dependence. Thus, the backtest masks the real performance characteristics of the system. In other words, fewer DF and a good backtest performance means the system is more valid. But more DF makes the test suspect; hence, the system's performance is not reflective of reality.

DF is expressed mathematically as

$DF=n-r,$

where n is the number of observations, and r is the number of relations.

So, n would be the number of data points, or historical prices in the backtest; r is a bit trickier to understand. One way to calculate DF is to use n as price points and r as rules combined with the data points used to calculate those rules. Hence, if one uses five years of closing prices, then $n=1,200$. If the system is a simple trend-following system that buys on a breakout of a fifty-day Donchian channel and a fifty-day Bollinger band, $r=52$ (fifty days and the Donchian rule, plus 1 for the Bollinger band rule; data points used up twice are counted as one). So, $DF=1,148$.

This backtest seems "free" enough. However, the exit has not been included. This type of system usually features a trailing stop, which is most commonly based on another moving average. However, this moving average would be enacted once an open position has been established. The trailing stop and its moving average would eat up more DF. Any additional rules or tweaks would further lower the DF. Whereas the trailing stop makes a significant difference in the performance of the system, adding more filters to the two-rule entry merely would likely make the system more brittle.

This simple system was traded successfully by the author in its simple form many years ago. In its original form, the system had the two entry rules and a long-term trailing stop (e.g., 100-day moving average). The entry rule parameters (channel lookback period and the moving average period for the Bollinger band) were optimized on a data set of thirty futures markets over a twenty- to fifty-year historical price period. No other filters were added. Hence, this system was very robust, that is, it had significant DF; and the test results showed strong profits, a choppy but rising equity curve, and a low Calmar ratio. The test results were mirrored in real time; over a six-year period, the system generated roughly 15 percent returns with a 25 percent max drawdown.

The lure of system trading for many beginner traders is the iterative backtesting procedure. New rules are added iteratively after a backtest in an attempt to isolate bad trades and capture more profitable trades. The problem is that the trader is "looking ahead" or "data snooping" and thereby restricting the data (lowering DF). He or she might try hundreds of different rules or combinations. The problem is that each new rule tested on the same data takes one degree of freedom away. Each new parameter, rule, exit, and other filters quickly adds up; and in one backtesting session, a trader could erase 3–400 degrees of freedom, leaving him or her with very little confidence in the trading system.

> The easiest way to overfit systems is to use hard-dollar stops and profit targets.
> Another great way to overfit is to use limit orders. This danger is especially relevant to high-frequency, countertrend systems. If you must use them, backtest to only trade when the historical price trades through the limit price.
> When adding indicators or filters, try to select ones that are lowly correlated—for example, do not use a RSI and a stochastic; rather, use a RSI and a moving average.
> Using more data, especially if the data represent the various modes of the market (i.e., uptrend, downtrend, sideways), does indeed help.
> Keeping a system simple (leaving more DF) helps as well. Scientists measure the extent to which a model is simple with the principle of parsimony, which is based on Occam's Razor (lexparsimonae), which states that "entities should not be multiplied unnecessarily." Indicator piling and adding rules to the same data via iterative backtesting are both violations of this principle.

Thus, watching DF will significantly help to build a better trading system. However, even with a large data set, another significant problem plagues backtesting. Data is replete with noise, that is, random price movements that exhibit no general pattern of behavior. There is no order or organization in this component of the price. If a system is optimized to the noise in the data, it is essentially learning or being developed on market patterns that will *never* be repeated again (as noise is random).

NOISE-FITTING (NF)

Although no specific term exists, NF might be a useful term to describe the process by which a system is developed on noise inherent in the backtesting data. It is safe to assume that any set of historical data will have enough noise to make this issue highly problematic. One could argue that all types of information expressed in a general time series will contain some noise and some signal components.

NF is best seen from a digital signal processing (DSP) point of view. DSP is used most widely in telecommunications, where the actual data sent over cable lines or through the air is a mix of both noise and signal. The noise represents the static that is heard, while the signal represents conversation, or the informational component. The ability to separate the two and then filter out the noise is of obvious benefit. Market prices are similar in that information is being conveyed in discrete time symbols, and random effects are built at each increment.

What happens when NF occurs is that the curve is being fit to the noise component in the data to a greater extent than the signal component. Some NF is obviously inevitable, but too much of it becomes a problem. For example, think of the noise as the random, whipsaw movements in the market and the signal as true trending movements. Hence, the signal component represents some type of repeatable pattern. Of course, a graphical representation of market prices (i.e., a price chart) will mask the components. The difficulty in delineating each part means that simple backtests will fit the system to varying amounts of noise. This noise component, being random, will not be repeated in the future; hence, the system becomes useless.

One important implication of NF is that the all-popular multimarket test is insufficient as a backtest procedure. Unfortunately, the majority of system traders seem to believe that a system tested on multiple markets can be considered reliable or robust systems. No matter how much data one has, there will be lots of noise. In fact, the more data, the greater the noise on an absolute basis. Hence, a single, simple backtest on massive amounts of data can also create NF and lead to bad trading systems.

Thus, the only sure way to backtest properly is to test a finalized system on data it has never seen before. This out-of-sample (OOS) data will have new noise that is not the same as the in-sample (INS) data on which it was developed. If the OOS results are similar to the INS results, then one can be confident in the system's predictive power. This method of testing predictive models is called *cross-validation*.

CROSS-VALIDATION

The importance of cross-validation (CV) cannot be overstated. It is clear that profits generated during a backtest on noise in the historical data will disappear in OOS data. Such a system will not generate profits in real time. A system that does well on OOS data, using the same optimal parameter set, stands a much better chance at stable future profits. CV provides a scientific method by which a trader can negate the effects of NF.

CV is a method of evaluating models by dividing the data into INS and OOS data sets. A system is backtested and its parameters optimized on the INS data. The optimal system is then tested as is on the OOS. The two performance data are compared. If the system was overfit to the INS data, it will show up in the inferior results of the OOS test. Think of the OOS period as the real-time data. Thus, CV provides the best estimate of how a trading system will do in real time. Because the noise component in the OOS data will be different, CV is able to isolate the "signal capturing" capabilities of our system for better evaluation.

This simplest version of CV is called the *holdout method*. Instead of using the entire backtesting historical data set at once, a small portion (e.g., 20%) is set aside. This OOS data is used after all the testing and optimization is done to test the final version of the system. The holdout method is simple—and better than a single backtest. However, this method has high variance; whichever data end up in the INS and OOS will cause large differences in performance.

For example, if a basic trend-following system had been optimized on the twenty-four months of daily data from January 2006 to December 2007 for the crude oil and then tested it on the first half of 2008 as the holdout period, the results may have turned out decent. If, instead, the system had started six months later and optimized on data from June 2006 to June 2008 and then tested on the second half of 2008 as the holdout period, the system would have likely tested very poorly.

The market changed dramatically during the second test (the market dropped from $150 to $40), making the parameters out of sync with the market during the OOS period. This sharp difference in data would have led to poor results and, perhaps, unduly cast the system in a bad light. The first test would have been more indicative of the system's long-term performance, because the OOS period was similar (but different enough) to the two years prior.

One improvement would be to conduct numerous holdout tests and then combine all the OOS period's performance; that would provide a much more comprehensive picture of the system's performance. This procedure is called *k-fold cross-validation* (KCV). In KCV, the historical data set is partitioned into multiple, equally sized segments of OOS segments to test on. For example, if the entire data set is five years, one would segment the data in 20 percent increments, or increments of one year. The system would then be optimized on the other four years (INS data) and then tested on the one remaining year (OOS data). The one year of OOS would rotate from year 1 to year 5, as shown in figure 1.

	Entire Historical Backtest Data				
	1994-5	1996-7	1998-9	2000-1	2002-3
Backtest 1	OOS	INS			
Backtest 2	INS	OOS	INS		
Backtest 3	INS		OOS	INS	
Backtest 4	INS			OOS	INS
Backtest 5	INS				OOS

Figure 1

The OOS results of each of the backtests can be combined and summarized to mimic real-time trading throughout the entire data set. By averaging, one can also get rid of some of the sensitivity to the location of the partition and get more generalized results. Note that the OOS period covers every bar of data in the backtest data set and thus provides a picture of how the system performs under varying market conditions. Again, if the averaged results are good, one would have a very robust system indeed.

The drawback to both the holdout and KCV is that they assume the market is static. In KCV, the INS and OOS periods are segmented in an orderly, if arbitrary, manner. If the market had progressed into a different price level over that period of time, a better way would have been to optimize on a prior period and then test it on a period immediately following. The backtest would then move forward and do the same, continuing on throughout all the data into the present and future in real-time trading. Testing would thus allow our system to optimize to changing market conditions. If the system was good, it would be able to adapt periodically and maintain its profitability throughout the entire backtest period.

WALK-FORWARD TESTING (WF)

This type of cross-validation is commonly called *walk-forward testing* (WF). WF not only provides a more effective testing procedure that can eliminate OF and NF, it also makes the system adaptive. That is, the parameters values of the indicators of the system are adapted to changing market conditions. This method uses the terms *training* and *testing* in lieu of INS and OOS, which assume a more static data set. The system is *trained* on the INS data, looking for the optimal parameters values of that data, and then the system is *tested* on the OOS data for validation.

The procedure moves forward a period, and the system is trained again on new data; if the market has changed, the parameter values will adapt/be trained to the new data and then tested again. A system that is validated thus and judged good can be traded in the same manner in real time. The test section becomes the future, where the system will be traded with its optimal parameter values.

In figure 2 below, an example is provided of how the segmentation and testing procedure is conducted. A five-year data set is segmented into a small piece of training data and a smaller piece of testing data. The size of the training data is highly discretionary and involves lots of trial and error. If one is trading a mid-term trend-following system, one year would probably be the minimum, as anything shorter would not generate enough trades to find statistically reliable optimal parameter values. The testing data size is usually between one-third and one-fifth of the training data set. This example chose three months, or 25 percent of the training data set. So the entire WF period is 1.25 years. This WF period is moved ahead three months at a time until the entire period is covered.

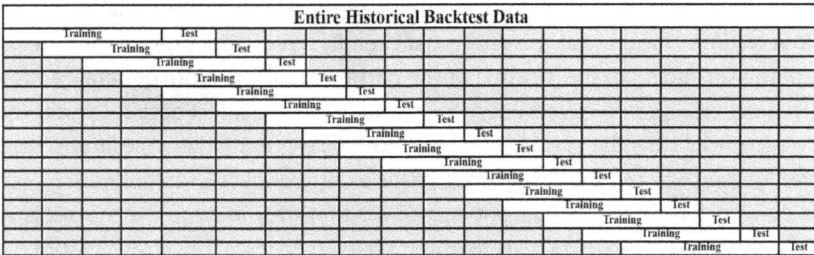

Entire Historical Backtest Data

(Diagram showing successive Training and Test blocks stepping forward through the data.)

Figure 2

The testing data can be combined in its original sequence, and the entire data set can be analyzed for performance. Positive results generated from NF will generally be eliminated. Also, if done correctly, the WF procedure itself can prevent unwanted OF via optimization of parameter values. Experienced system developers who use WF have found that near-optimal (as opposed to optimal) parameters that generalize better generate stronger performance in WF and real-time testing. For reliable performance, at minimum, some type of CV must be employed to validate a trading system. A WF testing procedure is the best way to do so. It assumes the constantly changing nature of the market and allows for some basic adaptation.

WF testing is an underdeveloped area, both in terms of its theory and practice. Much of its theoretical discussion misses the point on adaptation and reoptimization. Even experienced system traders are agnostic with regards to the nature of the market. Viewing the market as a static, linear mechanism would render systematic adaptation unnecessary. Hence, there is much confusion on this issue within the system trading community. To be fair, WF testing is much more difficult in practice than presented here. Indeed, much of its practice is conducted behind closed (and locked!) doors, as the technology and expertise needed to conduct WF testing on a regular basis in an efficient and effective manner are costly and difficult.

REOPTIMIZING

Many experienced system traders say that all (static) systems will die at some point. What they are saying is that no matter how good a system is now, it will eventually see some market condition that it cannot handle well. In effect, it is being killed off by natural selection, because it has no way to adapt (there is no adaptive mechanism built into the system) to the new condition. Hence, the adaptation offered by WF testing is key to the survival of a system. Many of these traders are of the opinion that systems should not be reoptimized but rather traded in their original form, including the same parameter values, continually.

However, assuming the markets change, reoptimization should be a core part of any trading system. If a market is trading in an entirely new price range, different from the historical data the system was developed on, parameter values should reflect this change (e.g., a $500 stop may work when crude oil is trading at $30, but will generate steady losses when crude oil is trading at $130). Many other aspects or signatures of the market may change dramatically, rendering the older parameter values out of sync.

The next chapter provides examples of OOS testing and adaptive trading systems using WF as a reoptimization procedure as well as a genetic algorithm system that also adapts the trading rules themselves. Before that discussion, one final comment must be made on reoptimization.

CHAPTER 8. ADAPTIVE SYSTEMS

This chapter provides examples of systems of progressively greater adaptability. It begins with a basic system and demonstrates the necessity of proper backtesting via KCV. An example of proper KCV backtesting is demonstrated, followed by a discussion and example of how WF is superior to KCV. Throughout this discussion, the necessity and benefits of reoptimization are reiterated.

Having a WF procedure to systematically and scientifically reoptimize and adapt a trading system is generally good enough. However, WF does confine itself to the reoptimization and adaptation of the system's parameter values only. A genetic algorithm (GA) system would take that adaptation a giant step forward by adapting the rules of the system as well, and an example of such a system is provided. The progression follows a simple trend-following system trained and tested on crude oil (WTI Crude Oil traded on the Nymex).

BASIC SYSTEM

This trend-following system trades on daily bars and goes long/short when the following conditions are met:

1) The close is higher/lower than the highest/lowest close of n bars ago (Donchian trend indicator)
2) Yesterday's short-term moving average is above/below that of three days ago (trend filter)
3) Yesterday's long-term moving average is above/below that of three days ago (trend filter)
4) The short-term moving average is above the long-term moving average (vice versa, trend filter)
5) The close is above/below the upper/lower Bollinger bands (whipsaw filter)

The system used hard-dollar, stop-loss, and profit-target orders to exit. All the system's parameters were optimized, including the Bollinger band parameters (averaging period and standard deviation). This system was intentionally OF to mimic the iterative optimization many system traders undertake. So what was the result?

The system was backtested on CL (historical back-adjusted) data from 1994 to 2003. This period exhibited both up- and downtrends. Heeding the consensus among system traders, due to the variety and length of the data, the backtest should provide reliable results. The system looks very promising indeed. Overall, the system was able to catch big chunks, as crude oil ran up in a strong uptrend. It got out quickly on bad trades with tight stops and took healthy profits.

Chart 1

Overall the system made $55,070 on 52 trades, with a maximum drawdown of -$2,750 (trade close to trade close). The system has a Calmar Ratio of 2.00 and a profit factor of 4.53. This system is highly profitable and has a fairly smooth equity curve.	Here is the equity curve of this system:

So if a trader had decided that this system was valid and decided to go ahead and trade over the next three years, he or she would have been disappointed. From 2004 to 2006, the system was unable to continue its rapid ascent in profits.

Chart 3

The system did manage to generate $7,160 in profits with a -$2,860 max drawdown over the three-year period; this performance would drop the system's Calmar Ratio to below half of the backtest's performance (0.83). 2004 was a similar period to the back-test data, and all the profits for the three years were made during that period. During 2005 and 2006, the system lost -$2,170, with a drawdown of -$2,860. Considering the lengthy range-bound market of 2005, the system did avoid taking large losses. 2006 provided a strong downtrend, which the system was unable to capitalize on. Further testing would show that the system was indeed biased to the upside, as it did well in 2007, but lost heavily during the subprime meltdown in 2008 (many system traders had records profits during this strong downtrend).

After ten years of strong performance, this system would have limped along over the next few years. In fact, if backtested on fifteen years of data (the original ten years used as INS data and the subsequent five used as OOS data), the system's equity curve would have looked like this:

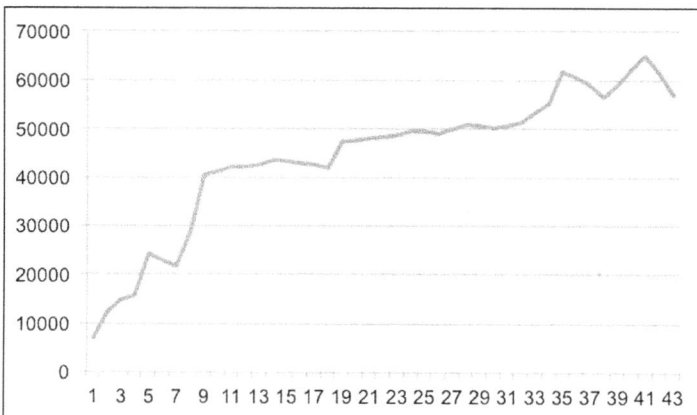

Chart 4

127

Take a good look at this equity curve, as this type of equity curve is typical of an over-fit system. Over the entire period, 95 percent of the profits of the system were made during the backtest period. Here is an equity curve of the latter five years:

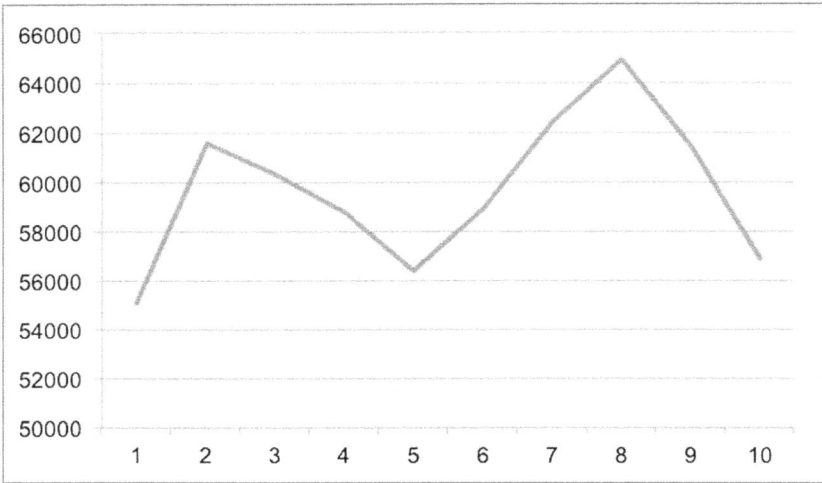

Chart 5

As can be seen, this system is hit-and-miss over the five years, in spite some of the strongest up- and downtrends this market has ever seen. If the market were to go into an extended range period, this system would likely lose significantly. This system is obviously overfit, and the problem is that the backtesting procedure was unable to catch the overfit nature of the system *before* live trading.

K-FOLD CROSS-VALIDATION

Might a KCV procedure have caught the problem before live trading commenced? To perform the KCV, the original ten years of data are divided into five 2-year periods. The system is then trained (the parameters are optimized) on four periods (INS data) and then tested on the one remaining period (OOS data). The results of the OOS periods are strung together to come up with the total performance.

Here is how the data is segmented:

	CL Continuous Back-Adjusted 1991 - 2000				
	1994-5	1996-7	1998-9	2000-1	2002-3
Backtest 1	OOS / Test	INS / Training			
Backtest 2	INS	OOS	INS		
Backtest 3	INS		OOS	INS	
Backtest 4	INS			OOS	INS
Backtest 5	INS				OOS

Here is a summary of the results:

	INS Training Period Optimal Parameters Values*	INS Training Performance (Profit, MaxDD, Calmar Ratio, Profit Factor)	OOS Test Performance
Backtest 1	8/60/12/60/25/25/20/2/ 1000/300/4200/500	$34,750 / -$3,845 / 1.13 / 2.75	-$1,140 / -$1,156 / NA / NA
Backtest 2	10/70/9/60/25/25/20/2/ 500/ 250/4800/500	$28,830 / -$3,855 / 0.93 / 2.75	$1,840 / -$2,010 / 0.46 / 1.61
Backtest 3	10/70/8/70/25/15/20/2 /1500/ 500/3800/500	$28,070 / -$4,425 / 0.79 / 2.79	$3,270 / -$4,410 / 0.74 / 1.54
Backtest 4	13/75/7/50/20/25/20/2/ 600/350/4600/400	$29,050 / -$4,265 / 0.85 / 2.88	-$1,410 / -$5,900 / NA / NA
Backtest 5	12/60/12/50/15/20/ 1250/250/6000/550	$42,280 / -$3,240 / 1.63 / 4.63	-$790 / -$5,520 / NA / NA

* Short and Long MAs for Long Trades, Short and Long MAs for Short Trades, Donchian Period for Long Trades, Donchian Period for Short Trades, Bollinger Band period and standard deviation, Stop Loss for Long Trades, Stop Loss for Short Trades, Profit Target for Long Trades, Profit Target for Short Trades.

By combining the OOS test results, a much more realistic picture of what this system will do in real-time trading emerges. The results are dramatically different from the original backtested performance. With a discrepancy this large, one can easily conclude that this system is not a profitable trading system. Similar to the earlier OOS tests, this system does not generate significant profits over an extended period of time. Further, the poor performance demonstrates the dangers of overfitting once again.

Original Backtest Performance	Combined OOS of k-fold CV Test
Net Profit: $55,070	Net Profit: $1,770
Max DD: -$2,750	Max DD: -$5,900
Calmar Ratio: 2.00	Calmar Ratio: NA
Profit Factor: 4.53	Profit Factor: NA
Chart 6	Chart 7

The good news is that KCV has been shown to be a powerful tool in testing systems. Of course, the system was designed intentionally to overfit the historical data. However, the basic system itself could be invalid and unable to generate profits. By simplifying and making a few tweaks to make the system more robust and a little more adaptive, one can better evaluate the system. If the tweaks help, then it was very likely overfit. In that case, by generalizing better, a trader should be able to develop a profitable system.

WHAT IS GOOD PERFORMANCE, ANYWAY?

Before improving the system, it might be useful to discuss exactly what type of performance one wants. In the real world, trading performance is generally a lot worse—and certainly more nuanced—than the popular media depicts. The only rational way to judge one's performance is to compare one's system to other successful trading systems or system traders.

This list is comprised of some of the top CTA programs in the United States; programs less than five years old were excluded. These programs have thrived with consistently strong performance through some of the most diverse market conditions. They represent a good snapshot of what the best system traders are capable of (indeed, the performance represented here mirror the performances of the best hedge fund managers worldwide).

Name	Compound RoR	Max DD	Calmar Ratio
Mesirow Financial Commodities Absolute Return Strategy	12.49%	-1.77%	7.06
Covenant Capital Management Original	14.75%	-28.61%	0.52
Quantum Leap Capital Mgmt	23.34%	-24.45%	0.95
Chesapeake Capital Diversified Program	13.53%	-23.36%	0.51
Clarke Capital Management Worldwide	15.29%	-26.06%	0.58
NuWave Investment Combined Futures	12.64%	-17.01%	0.74

Figure 6

The return profiles differ with some aggressive managers with higher RoRs and Max DDs, as well as lower RoRs and lower Max DDs. What is common to all, with the exception of the Mesirow program, is that it is difficult to maintain Calmar Ratios above 1.50. Strong returns demand taking risk and absorbing high volatility. The market rewards investors who can deal with uncertainty about future performance. Investors wanting to know exactly how much and when future returns will come from will have to settle for the CD provided at the local bank.

One other note is that the longest performing managers (Clarke Capital, Chesapeake, NuWave) tend to have lower Calmar Ratios. Further research into the performance of the top managers in any asset class will show that maintaining a Calmar Ratio near 1.00 over 10+ years is quite a feat of excellence; maintaining a Calmar Ratio over 0.50 while generating 20% returns is just as difficult. There are very few managers who can accomplish this feat. Incidentally, this general feature of investing would indicate that the younger managers on this list will see their Calmar Ratios gradually heading south over the next five to six years.

Thus, the results from the basic system's original backtest were fantastical in comparison. In spite of the hard-won reality provided by top investors over the past fifty years, many investors still seek myriad holy grails of exaggerated performance, such as high returns (e.g., above 15 %) with minimal volatility (e.g., max DD below 10%) and an unrealistically smooth equity curve. If a diversified portfolio of great systems by the leading CTAs cannot attain these results, one cannot expect one's own trading system to do so.

BASIC SYSTEM 2.0

From the outset it would be prudent to adjust expectations to a realistic level. A good trend-following system, trading one contract at a time, would make at least 10 percent returns per year, with a generally rising equity curve, a max drawdown of less than 20 percent, and a minimum Calmar Ratio of 0.50. Most importantly, the system should not be overfit; the system should be robust, generalized to many different types of trends in the market. In other words, the system should generate profits similar to that indicated in the backtest and on a consistent basis.

To achieve these goals, the system must be improved. As mentioned before, hard-dollar stops and profit targets are one of the best ways to OF. Hence, these are the first components to change. Another easy way to OF is to use too much granularity in the parameter values. A robust system will work just as well with a twelve-day moving average as with a thirteen-day moving average. However, to backtest using a parameter range that searches in increments of 1 will overfit the system to that single moving average and make a bad system look a lot better than it actually is. To prevent this danger, rough parameter increments will be used.

Our stop-losses will be changed to an ATR (average true range)-based stop à la Chuck Lebeau. Simply, the system will "hang" a stop-loss order equal to two times the 10-bar ATR from the point of entry. This stop will not follow favorable price movements but will remain at its original price. Profit targets will be scrapped in favor of a trailing stop. This system will use a simple 20-bar moving average that is triggered once the market has moved one 10-bar ATR in a favorable direction from the entry price.

As opposed to the hard-dollar amounts, the use of price ranges allows for much greater adaptability and prevents the severe OF of hard-dollar targets. Similarly, the beauty of a trailing stop is not only that it allows for profits to ride but also that it reflects several different changes in price action. Hence, a moving average that follows the trend works in many different types of trends (though not all—e.g., sharp reversals that occur within a shorter window than the lookback period of the moving average will generate smaller profits).

One of the trickier aspects of incorporating CV into backtesting is parameter selection. After backtesting on INS data, a trader will find numerous different parameters sets that work. Each generate slightly different results, with some generating more profits, some smaller drawdowns; all the usual statistical characteristics can be calculated for each parameter set. Some parameter sets will also curve fit more than others. So which parameter set should be selected for OOS testing and live trading? *The parameter set that generates the optimal performance while overfitting the least is best.* In the first backtest, the parameter set with the highest net profit was chosen. However, the highest net profit seldom indicates the best parameter set for future performance. It is produced from too many random variables in the data and is highly susceptible to OF.

It takes a great deal of experience and research to develop one's own method. But in general, extremely well-performing parameter sets should be avoided. A Calmar Ratio above one is difficult to sustain, so parameter sets with high Calmars should be suspect. Another statistic to watch for is number of trades. Generally speaking, a backtest should contain enough trades across the entire data set to provide an objective evaluation of the system. What constitutes enough varies greatly on the type of system, market, and time frame. However, generally, when choosing a parameter set, a set that generates more trades is better.

The parameter set criteria used here is the same one used in the WF testing in the next section. To isolate the best performing par sets, the bottom 25 percent max drawdown sets, any parameter set with a max drawdown over -$10,000 and net profit under $35,000 are eliminated. Also, to avoid OF parameter sets, the highest 25 percent net profit sets as well as sets with a profit factor over 3.00, Calmar Ratio over 1.50, are eliminated. From the remaining sets, the parameter set with the highest number of trades is chosen.

For now, a simple backtest on INS and OOS data should provide some early indications of the system's effectiveness. On the original data set from 1994 to 2003, Basic System 2.0 with its optimal parameter set (using the criteria outlined above) generated $42,010 net profit on twenty-nine trades with a maximum drawdown of -$5,430 (INS). The system has a Calmar Ratio of 0.28 and a profit factor of 2.23. The equity rises but is not the smoothest.

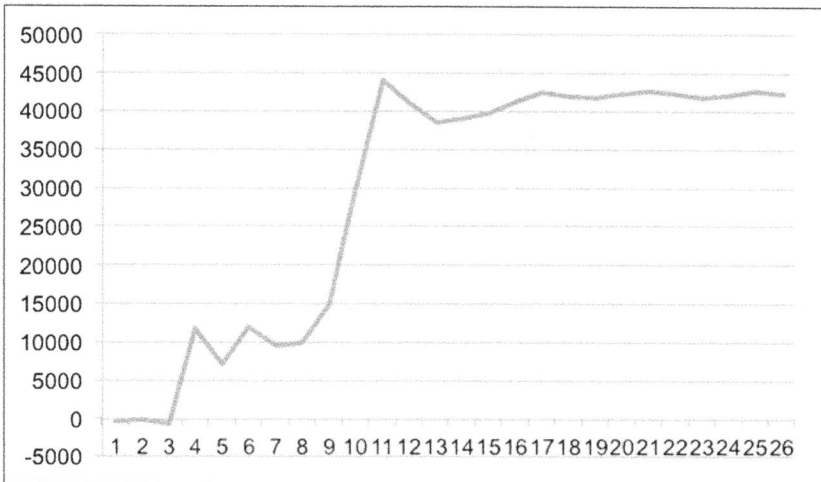

Chart 8

How did the system do on the next three years (OOS data)? Using this same parameter set over OOS data from 2004 through 2006, the system managed to eke out almost $10,000. Not bad, but hardly a great system. Of note is that the system struggled through the OOS period, but instead of losing, it simply did not trade, indicating that the filter was working to keep it out of the market during sideways range markets.

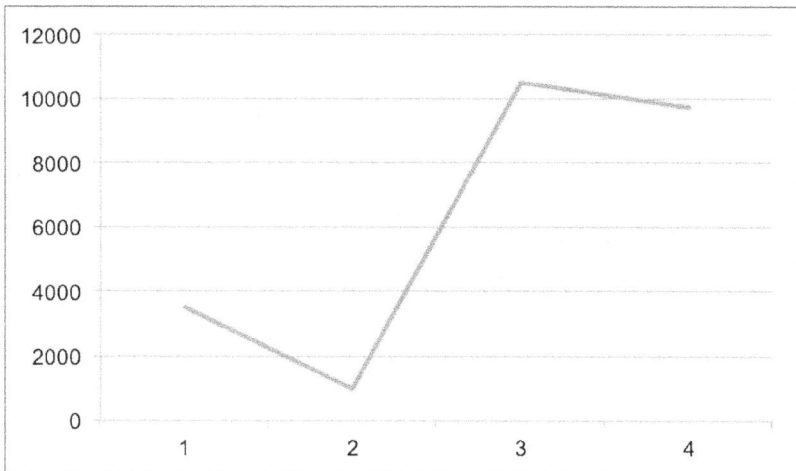

Chart 9

Testing this system on the next five years of OOS data through the end of 2008, the system was able to recover. As shown in the equity curve, as trends emerged, the system started generating profits again. Over the next couple of years, it was able to capitalize on the volatility of 2007 and 2008 very well.

133

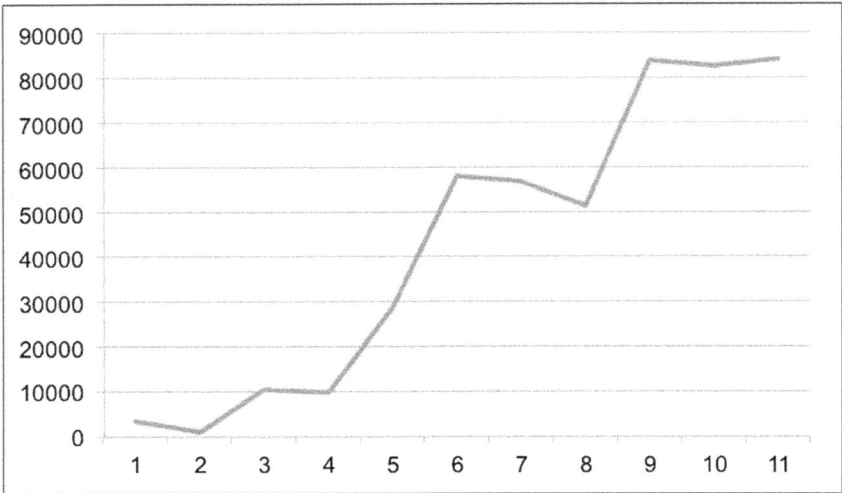

Chart 10

On the entire five years of OOS data (2004–2008), the system generated $84,170 net profits on eleven trades with a max drawdown of -$14,670. The Calmar Ratio was 1.15, and the profit factor was 5.81. Thus, this system is not by any measure a *great* system, but it works and looks to generate enough profits on a consistent basis, based on initial testing. At the very least, this system is not overfit, as the first system was, and should be robust enough to capture long trends. Now this system will be tested using KCV testing.

KCV TESTING OF BASIC SYSTEM 2.0

In this KCV, the same criteria from above to select the best parameter sets will be used. It will be used for each test to select the optimal parameter set of each period (which will likely be different). Again, these criteria will seek to choose the parameter set that generates the best performance while overfitting the least. The same period segmentation from the previous test is used.

Parameter Selection Criteria		INS Training Period Optimal Parameters Values*	INS Training Performance (Profit, MaxDD, Calmar Ratio, Profit Factor)	OOS Test Performance
Filter out parameter sets w/ following characteristics > Bottom 25% max drawdown > Max drawdown over -$10,000 > Highest 25% net profit > Profit factor over 3.00 > Calmar Ratio over 1.50 > Select parameter set with the highest number of trades Parameters will be optimized thus: LMA1Per: 10-50x20 LMA2Per: 50-150x25 SMA1Per: 10-50x20 SMA2Per: 50-150x25 DonchPer: 50-150x25 BBPer: 50-150x25 StanDev: 1-3x1	Backtest 1	10/50/10/150/50/75/1	$14,430/-$8,425/0.21/1.64/	$1,270/-$1,970/0.32/1.64
	Backtest 2	10/75/10/150/50/50/2	$7,610/-$4,433/0.29/1.51	$6,1250/-$5,120/0.58/2.20
	Backtest 3	30/50/10/125/100/50/2	$8,998/-$6,578/0.17/1.87	$5,910/N/A/N/A/N/A *This parameter set generated only four trades, all of which were winners. The intraday MaxDD was -$4,410.
	Backtest 4	10/50/50/125/50/75/2	$20,540/-$9,645/0.27/2.49	$6,150/-$4,720/0.65/2.30
	Backtest 5	10/50/50/125/50/75/1	$28,710/-$9,645/0.37/2.28	$4,480/N/A/N/A/N/A *This parameter set generated only four trades, all of which were winners. The intraday MaxDD was -$11,650.

Here is a summary comparison of the backtested results and the combined results of the KCV test.

The KCV test results for the improved system generate less profits, but with far lower volatility, as the Calmar Ratio is three times higher than the original INS backtest. The equity curve steadily rises without being OF. This system is profitable and robust and should generate consistent profits going forward.

Original Backtested (INS) Performance	Combined OOS of KCV Test
Net Profit: $42,010	Net Profit: $23,185
Max DD: -$5,430.	Max DD: -$4,350
Calmar Ratio: 0.28	Calmar Ratio: 0.97
Profit Factor: 2.23	Profit Factor: 2.15

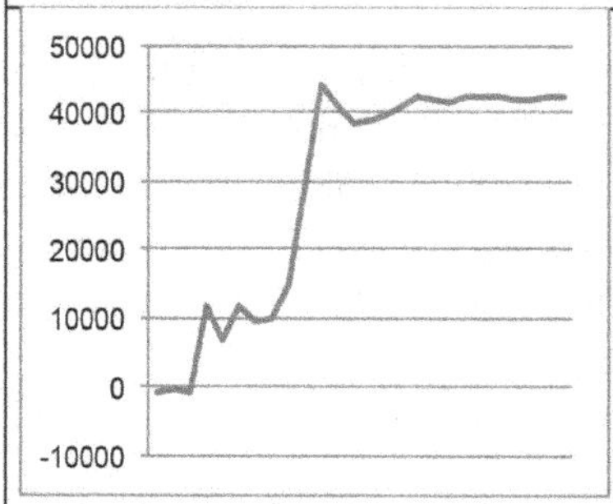

Chart 11

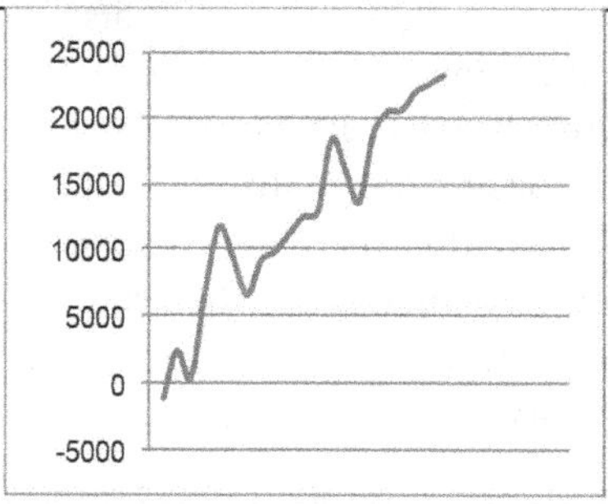

Chart 12

WF TESTING EXAMPLE

In spite of the usefulness of KCV, it has two significant deficiencies. The procedure itself does not provide for a parameter set that is the optimal one to use *going forward* (or at all, for that matter). Because the training and test periods are chosen arbitrarily, there is no practical answer as to how a system should be traded in real time.

The second problem is that the system is static. Once tested and judged a profitable system, the one optimal parameter set must be used for the lifetime of the system. If the market becomes significantly different, the system may not survive. More pertinently, significant price changes (e.g., subprime crisis period) provide different patterns and opportunities; the old parameter set will become suboptimal if markets move into new price territory.

Instead of arbitrarily choosing an OOS test section, a WF test "walks forward" the OOS section one increment at a time, using the preceding periods as the INS training period, as outlined in figure 2 above. In this example, the system is trained on two years of data and then tested on the following six months of data, for a 4:1 ratio of INS to OOS data. Moving forward allows the system to adapt to increasing price and volatility levels, as well as changing signatures accompanying range and trend modes.

Specifically, one of the problems that arises from the opportunities of this data set is that the uptrend of 2006–2007 and the downtrend of 2008 are too strong. An optimized trend-following system should be able to make significant profits in a short period of time with low volatility. A system optimized towards sideways markets will have longer parameter values to filter out the whipsaws, but this would also cause it to enter late and thereby be unable to maximize profits during these kinds of trends.

The other problem is that a system optimized for an uptrend will make it easier to go long and harder to go short; hence, traders would miss out on much of the subsequent crash. A robust trading system would forgo much of the profits here to generalize more toward larger patterns. However, if such abrupt changes stayed consistent, this system would have a rough two to three years.

Using the same selection criteria as the previous KCV test to select the optimal parameter set, the WF procedure was able to both lower risk during the choppy 2005 period and capitalize on the sharp trends and reversals of the subprime crisis period. During the 2005 period, the system adapted by widening the Bollinger bands to lower the frequency of the trades and then shortened them during 2007 to enter trends faster. The other parameters values reacted similarly.

To make a fair comparison, the KCV testing was extended through the end of 2008.

Entire Historical Backtest Data

Training		Test															
	Training		Test														
		Training		Test													
			Training		Test												
				Training		Test											
					Training		Test										
						Training		Test									
							Training		Test								
								Training		Test							
									Training		Test						
										Training		Test					
											Training		Test				
												Training		Test			
													Training		Test		
														Training		Test	
															Training		Test

The results are clearly in favor of the WF method of testing and trading the system. On comparing the two charts, one can see key differences in the way each traded. As the trend strengthened, the parameters shortened in order to enter trends early. Hence, the WF procedure chose a tighter parameter set, which allowed the system to enter the market sooner. Of course, had the sharp uptrend during the latter half of 2007 been slower, the system would have entered the subsequent downtrend much later. The KCV tested system is using a parameter set that is more conservative, having been optimized with data that included the protracted range market of 2005. Hence, that system entered the market much later.

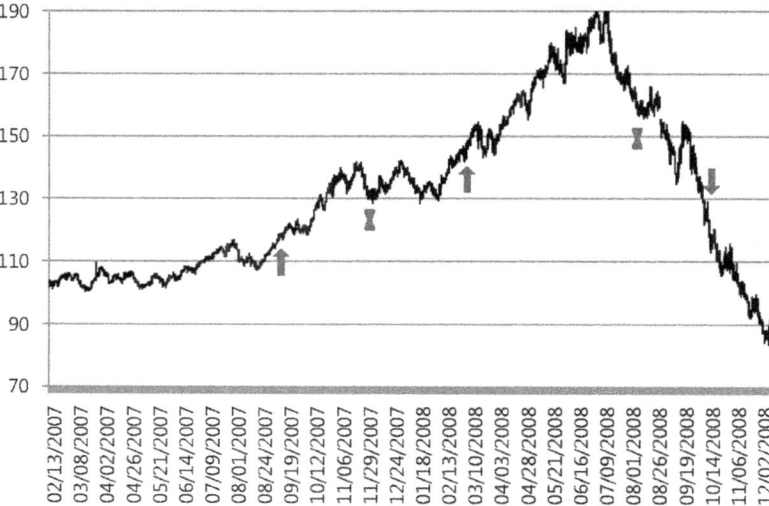

Chart 15: KCV OOS trades

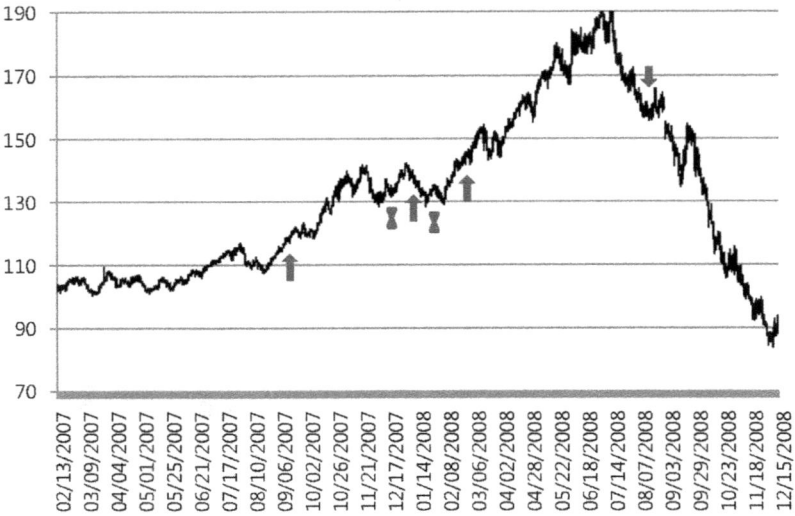

Chart 16: WF OOS Trades

Speaking of which, the choppy market of 2005 had one thing going for it: it was long. Hence, the adaptive system (the WF-optimized system) was able to adapt in time to lower losses. In the KCV test, the system was generally optimized for all the trends that had taken place before and after this period. Therefore, it did rather poorly during this time, getting whipsawed frequently. Had the range mode been shorter, the WF optimization would have likely led the system to increased losses.

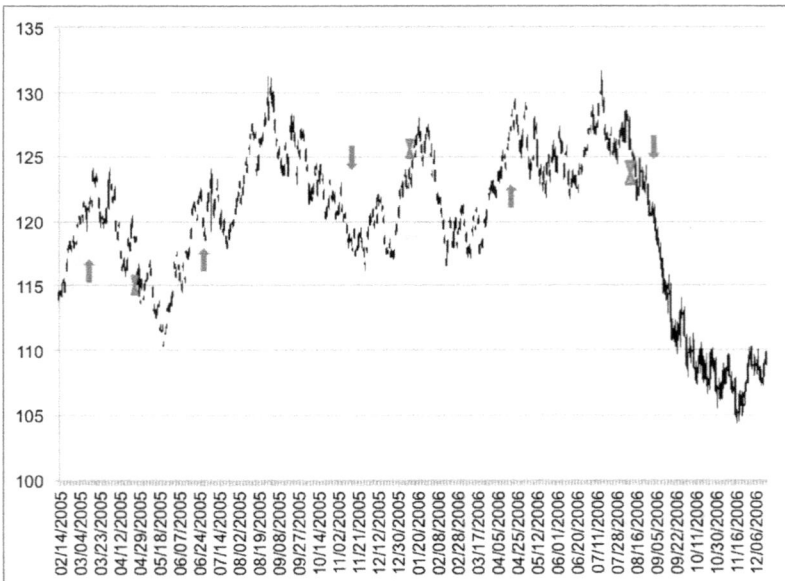

Chart 17: KCV OOS trades during 2005-2006

The adaptive system was able to adjust in the middle of 2005, widening the parameters to stay out of this market. It was able to avoid three losing trades from which the static version of the system (the KCV-optimized system) suffered. In exchange, the adaptive system entered the 2006 short trade later but still managed a profit. Overall, the WF-optimized system had a net gain of over $15,000 during this period, whereas the KCV-optimized system lost roughly $5,000 and also suffered through a year of whipsaw trades.

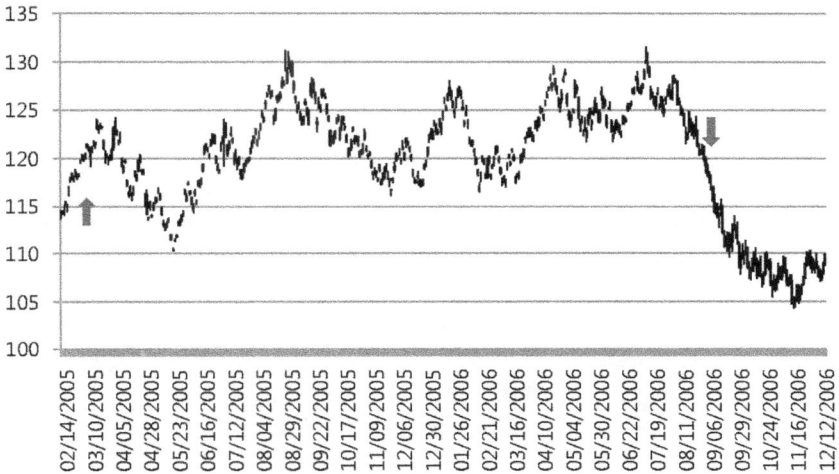

Chart 18

This is a very rough WF procedure; there are numerous ways it can be improved. Poorly designed WF procedures can generate false results:

> Studies have shown that a randomly chosen, poor or OF model can make money in one or two walk-forward tests. Studies have also shown, however, that such a model will not make money over a large number of walk-forward tests. Therefore, to achieve the greatest confidence, a series of walk-forward tests, or a *walk-forward analysis*, must be performed on a trading model. A trading model that makes a significant overall profit in a large number of walk-forward tests, where at least 50% of the tests are profitable, is likely to be successful.[103]

Although far from a holy grail, a WF procedure will provide a longer-lasting system and incremental improvements to its performance.

---

103   Robert Pardo, *Design, Testing and Optimization of Trading Systems* (Hoboken, NJ: Wiley, 1992). Pardo's book is the bible on correct backtest and optimization procedures and has an informative chapter on how to construct and implement walk-forward testing.

In sum, the WF test is a much more scientific and rational way to adapt to changing market conditions. Discretionary traders who rely on small numbers of observations and vague generalizations about market changes will make confused choices about how to adapt their trading activities. Moreover, there is no way to quantify the resulting performance with any confidence. Adding this level of adaptability to any valid trading system makes for a powerful combination of rigor and flexibility that will lead to longevity and confidence in investment activities.

GA EXAMPLE SYSTEM

Both versions of the basic system had a difficult time during 2005 and 2006. The problem is that two years is a long time to wait for profits to accrue again. Also, if that type of market pattern continues for even longer, the system might as well be considered dead. One solution is to come up with a new strategy that works during such periods. An even better solution is to let a GA find one.

In this example, similar to the WF procedure, a GA program will walk forward in time and develop new rules; that is, instead of just adapting parameters, the GA program will also adapt its rules as well. Ideally it will be able to evolve varying strategies, using the same universe of rules and indicators. Hopefully, it will be able to devise a countertrend, or perhaps a shorter-term trend-following system, to adapt to and profit from the long-range period of 2005–2006. Just as important, it should be able to adapt back to a trend-following system in 2007, so it does not miss the subsequent trends.

Thus far, one system was backtested on a data set, using two different methods. The KCV method was able to validate an entirely static system, where the rules and the parameter set remained the same. Then a WF method was able to validate a partially adaptive system, where the parameter set was adapted to current market conditions. In this test a fully adaptive method will walk forward in time and then summarize the results of the testing set (OOS data) to evaluate the system.

Specifically, the GA will adapt rules and parameters in the training period. Then the optimal system will be tested on the subsequent OOS period to evaluate its performance. Then the OOS results of all three methods will be compared over the same period. The GA in this example will draw from a small pool of indicators and rules used in Basic System 2.0, along with basic price values (open, high, low, close) and basic mathematical operators (plus, minus, multiplication, and division). To increase flexibility, the GA will be allowed to combine the indicators in a number of ways.

In a GA-generated system, the inputs can be practically anything that can be expressed numerically. Wise choices in inputs are often the difference between success and failure. In a larger sense, the inputs used are the constraints placed on the evolutionary search process. Instead of using wide-open evolution, starting from scratch—which would include a vast number of unnecessary candidates and an impractically long period of time—one can restrict the GA to search a much smaller, yet sufficiently diverse area of the solution space. One's knowledge of the Bollinger Band and experience of its success is acting as Dennett's crane, enabling one to leapfrog a vast number generations. This example has chosen to use the Bollinger Band as the only technical indicator for purposes of comparison.

The walk-forward windows will consist of a twelve-month training period and a three-month testing period, starting in 1994 and ending in 2010. Thus, the system will start by training both rule and parameter sets on the entire 1994 period, then test the optimal trading system on the first three months of 1995. Next, it will train a new system from April 1994 through April 1995 and test the optimal system of that period from April through June of 1995.

The same parameter set selection criteria from the WF example will be used here. In addition, a rule set selection criteria must be implemented. Here again, the best criteria is that which provides the best performance with the least amount of OF. To do so, the following four criteria will be used to select the best rule set:

1) Highest Calmar Ratio under six.[104]
2) Maximum Drawdown of less than $10,000.
3) Smoothest equity curve.
4) More than four trades, fewer than twenty trades.

In addition, the following two rules will be used to filter the vast number of profitable rule and parameter set combinations:

1) Robust parameter set. If a twenty-five-day moving average generates great returns, but a twenty-four-day moving average generates losses, the twenty-five-day moving average value is OF. That entire range of moving average values would be eliminated, and a range of values that all generate similarly good performance will be selected. By plotting the range of optimal parameter values versus the Calmar Ratio, the GA program can create a surface gradient for each parameter. OF parameter values will contain spikes rather than flat surfaces. So the GA will look for the lowest gradients and choose those parameter values.

2) Fewest terms in the rules (parsimony pressure). William of Ockham was right: the simpler the better. In general, rule sets that are simpler are better (more DF). Due to the GA's ability to combine different parts with others, even a small number of inputs can create an enormously large number of terms in rule sets, many of which only serve to OF the rule set to the training data. After all of the criteria listed above filter out undesirable rules and parameter sets, the system with the fewest terms will be the chosen optimal trading system.

---

104   The Calmar Ratio is normally calculated using the average return over the past three years. Here we will use an approximation based only on one year's net profit.

The rule sets the GA evolves will seem a bit strange. The GA is an algorithm for manipulating genes or building blocks into different combinations. Hence, the GA sees the Bollinger Band input as three different "genes"—the upper band, middle band/moving average, and the lower band. The varying lookback periods with which to calculate the Bollinger Band, as well as the varying standard deviations, represent still more building blocks. The GA then puts these pieces together, using mathematical operators in the form of a mathematical formula.

The formula spits out a number, which is then used to create an entry signal, normally in the form of a threshold value—which, if high enough, will generate a buy signal; and, if low enough, will generate a sell signal. For example, the rule sets might use the difference between one period's upper band and another period's upper band and then multiply the difference by the moving average. If this number is greater than, say, 50, it will buy; if lower than, say, 25, it will sell. This awkward language is due to the simplistic representation scheme of the GA. For purposes of simplicity, we will consider stop-and-reversal (SAR) strategies only so that a buy and sell represent entries, unless there is an open position, in which case a buy and sell represents an exit of the existing position and an entry in the opposite direction.

SUMMARY OF FIRST 15 RULE SETS

Period	Rule *Rules are summarized and interpreted for ease of understanding		Type of Strategy	Training Period (INS) Results	Testing Period (OOS) Results
	Actual	Interpretation & Comments			
1 (INS: 6/94-8/95; OOS: 7/95-9/95)	Divide difference between 25-day MA and LB of 50-day BB by LB of 100-day BB. If this term is greater than threshold value of 25, buy; if lower, then sell (think of threshold as indicator like RSI with upper and lower thresholds that trigger trades).	GA evolved counter-trend strategy that measured differences between MA and 2 bands. These lines separate during uptrends and move closer during downtrends.	CT	Net Profit: $8,390 Max DD: $3,550 Calmar: 2.36	Net Profit: $1,250 Max DD: $1,150 Calmar: N/A
2	Multiply 100-day UB by difference of 50-day LB and H. If term is greater than -20, buy; if lower than -65, then sell.	Another overbought/sold indicator using difference between high and LB. As market moves away from average and becomes more overbought, the difference between the two becomes greater. This is magnified by the UB, which stretches wider when overbought and drops quickly when oversold.	CT	Net Profit: $12,720 Max DD: $2,530 Calmar: 5.02	Net Profit: $3,500 Max DD: $675 Calmar: N/A
3	None met criteria; no trades	N/A	N/A	Net Profit: N/A Max DD: N/A Calmar: N/A	Net Profit: N/A Max DD: N/A Calmar: N/A
4	Divide greater of 50-day UB and 25-day UB by difference of 100-day UB and 50-day UB. Then multiply by 50-day UB. If term is greater than -25, then buy; if lower than -40, then sell.	By using 25, 50 and 100-day periods, GA creates oscillator that detects weakening trends. When trend begins to correct or congests, 25-day UB drops below other two, creating lower term value signaling sell.	CT Entry / TF Exit**	Net Profit: $15,530 Max DD: $2,850 Calmar: 5.86	Net Profit: $6,640 Max DD: $1,120 Calmar: N/A
5	None met criteria; no trades	N/A	N/A	Net Profit: N/A Max DD: N/A Calmar: N/A	Net Profit: N/A Max DD: N/A Calmar: N/A
6	If 100-day LB is greater than 30, buy; if lower, then sell.	Simple moving average trend-following system. The clean trends pushed the GA towards TF system; selected system was simplest.	TF	Net Profit: $19,570 Max DD: $3,850 Calmar: 5.36	Net Profit: $3,730 Max DD: $1,550 Calmar: N/A
7	Multiply difference of 25-day UB and Low by 100-day UB. If term is greater than 18, buy; if lower than -19, sell.	If UB is increasing quickly and separating from Low, indications of uptrend present and vice versa. This data set contained more congestion periods and hence needed system that allowed for flexible directional changes.	CT Entry / TF Exit	Net Profit: $18,890 Max DD: $5,580 Calmar: 3.40	Net Profit: $1,870 Max DD: $2,750 Calmar: N/A
8	Divide 25-day UB by difference of 100-day LB and 50-day LB. If greater than -22, buy; if lower than -68, sell.	Similar to moving average crossover, term gets greater as upswing in price drags up 25-day UB faster than slower-moving terms in denominator. The presence of one large trend in the training period and a large correction in the testing period made it difficult to generalize; hence the disparity in results.	TF	Net Profit: $15,950 Max DD: $3,850 Calmar: 4.14	Net Profit: -$1,350 Max DD: $3,210 Calmar: N/A

#	Rule	Commentary	Type	Result A	Result B
9	Multiply 100-MA by difference of 100-day UB and 25-day UB. If greater than 40, buy; if lower than -5, sell.	Moving-average crossover's differences are amplified so as to catch turning points. Training data included more uptrends. Hence, the threshold values were biased towards easier short entries to get in downtrends faster.	CT	Net Profit: $14,520 Max DD: $5,810 Calmar: 2.59	Net Profit: $250 Max DD: $3,250 Calmar: N/A
10	Divide 50-day UB by difference of 50-day MA and 25-day MA. Then add 25-day LB. If greater than 50, buy; if lower than -50, sell.	Pure counter-trend system: when overbought, 25-day MA rises faster making term value negative and vice versa. This market was range-bound and very choppy. GA developed a pure CT system, which also took advantage of GA's natural SAR trading scheme, making this system ideal for current market condition. Testing section was similar.	CT	Net Profit: $7,260 Max DD: $3,250 Calmar: 2.23	Net Profit: $4,420 Max DD: $1,230 Calmar: N/A
11	Multiply 25-day LB by difference of 100-day UB and 50-day UB. If greater than 55, buy; if lower than 35, sell.	Overbought conditions cause 50-day to rise more than 100-day, causing the term value to fall lower, thus generating sell signal. Generally choppy but more downtrends, hence, optimal threshold makes it easier to enter downtrends rather than uptrends.	CT	Net Profit: $8,080 Max DD: $3,120 Calmar: 2.59	Net Profit: $4,620 Max DD: $1,340 Calmar: N/A
12	Multiply 100-day UB by difference of 100-day MA and 50-day UB. If greater than -55, buy; if lower than -70, sell.	MA crossover at turning points.	CT Entry / TF Exit	Net Profit: $11,110 Max DD: $2,560 Calmar: 4.34	Net Profit: -$2,120 Max DD: $2,540 Calmar: N/A
13	None met criteria, no trades	N/A	N/A	Net Profit: N/A Max DD: N/A Calmar: N/A	Net Profit: N/A Max DD: N/A Calmar: N/A
14	None met criteria, no trades	N/A	N/A	Net Profit: N/A Max DD: N/A Calmar: N/A	Net Profit: N/A Max DD: N/A Calmar: N/A
15	Multiply 100-day MA by difference of 50-day LB and 25-day LB. If greater than -1.5, buy; if lower than -10, sell.	Market was in choppy downtrend for entire period. So difference between LBs were used to indicate overbought conditions with which to sell again.	TF/CT hybrid	Net Profit: $14,170 Max DD: $3,850 Calmar: 3.88	Net Profit: $3,030 Max DD: $1,280 Calmar: N/A

O=Open, H=High, L=Low, C=Close, MA=Moving Average, BB=Bollinger Band, UB=Upper Band of Bollinger Band, LB=Lower Band of Bollinger Band, CT=Counter-Trend, TF=Trend-Following

** When trends are quiet and persistent, the GA built in a longer-period, less sensitive entry to mimic a trailing stop by simply holding on to gains longer.

DISCUSSION OF RESULTS

The GA program took as an input the same Bollinger Band indicator and used this, along with the other price points, to generate optimized trading systems. With its ability to evolve different combinations of systems, the GA was able to develop strategies that took advantage of both trending and range-bound periods at varying levels of success. The WF Test system was able to choose parameters that avoided the range-bound periods (the second-best strategy), as the rules of that system were locked into a trend-following strategy. The GA systems were tested on OOS data, consisting of the data from the three-month period following the training period. In sum, greater profits and a smoother equity curve were generated by the GA program.

Combined OOS of k-fold CV Test 1994-2008	Combined OOS of WF Test 1994-2008	Combined OOS of GA Test 1994-2008
Net Profit: $66,985 Max DD: -$8,715 Calmar Ratio: 0.51 Profit Factor: 3.25	Net Profit: $126,450 Max DD: -$10,850 Calmar Ratio: 0.78 Profit Factor:6.85[1]	Net Profit: $195,780 Max DD: -$7,950 Calmar Ratio: 1.64 Profit Factor: 8.56[2]
Chart 19	Chart 20	Chart 21

*Equity curves are not scaled properly

The main reason for the GA's superior performance was its ability to adapt its rules to capitalize on both range and trending markets. Prices during 1994–1995 were range-bound, followed by trendy price action in 1996, only to be followed by range-bound price action in 1997. The following examples string together trades from successive OOS periods during the time frame indicated.

EXAMPLE 1: PERIOD 2 (SEE SUMMARY TABLE ABOVE)

9/1994–12/1995

This choppy range period persisted enough for the GA to adapt a countertrend strategy and then profit from it nicely.

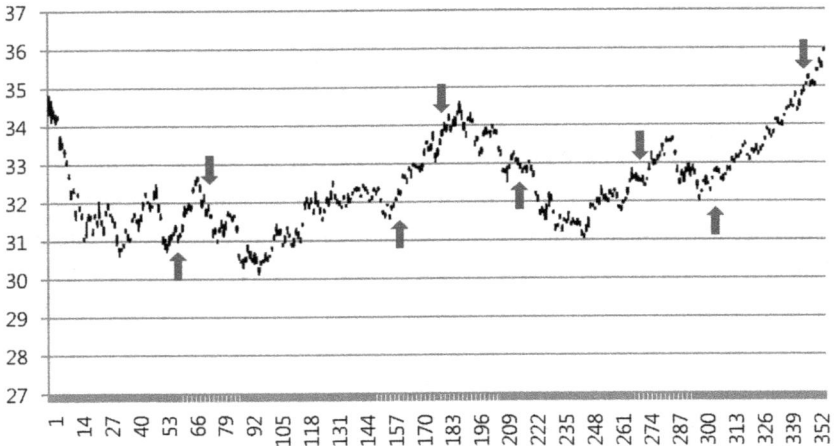

Chart 22

EXAMPLE 2: PERIOD 6

9/1995–11/1996

In lieu of a traditional MA trend-following system, the GA found the long-term LB a good indicator to get in and out of this strong uptrend.

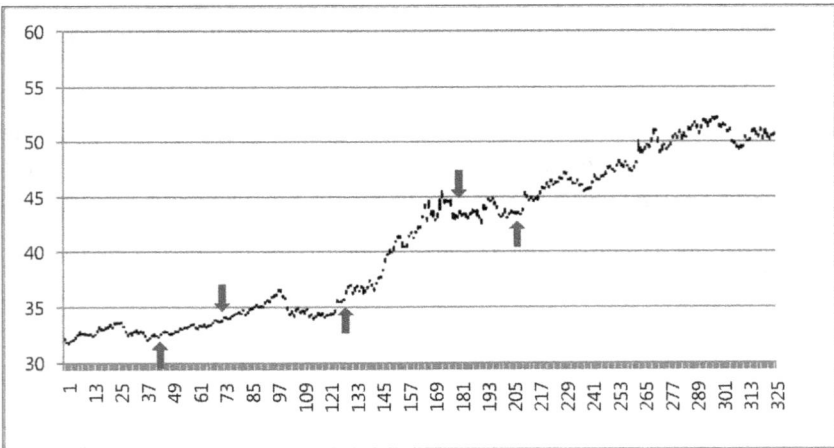

Chart 23

EXAMPLE 3: PERIOD 10

8/1996–10/1997

This market was characterized by severe choppiness, with both range-bound and trend modes. The GA was able to evolve a pure countertrend system that benefited from sharp, spiky moves up and down.

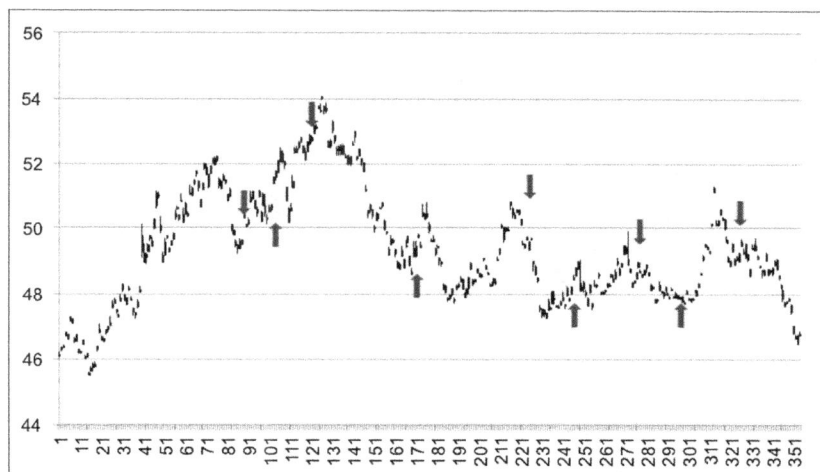

Chart 24

SUMMARY

This example system only used one common indicator, recombining each piece using an evolutionary heuristic. Walking forward in time, this system adapted not only its parameters but also its rules to better fit and profit from changing market conditions. This example was for illustrative purposes only and, hence, used an overly simple SAR approach to entries and exits. Full system development would have to employ protective stops and profits targets, including trailing stops, among other techniques to improve trading performance.

BIBLIOGRAPHY

Aronson, David. *Evidence-Based Technical Analysis.* Hoboken, NJ: Wiley, 2007.

Arthur, Brian. "Positive Feedbacks in the Economy." *Scientific American* (1990).

Arthur, Brian, J. H. Holland, B. LeBaron, R. Palmer, and P. Tayler. "Asset Pricing Under Endogenous Expectations in an Artificial Stock Market." SFI Paper 96-12-093, *Economic Notes* (1997).

Bak, Per, Ken Chan, Jose Scheinkman, and M. Woodford. "Self Organized Criticality and Fluctuations in Economics." Santa Fe: Santa Fe Institute, 1992.

Beinhocker, Eric. *The Origin of Wealth.* Boston: Harvard Business School Press, 2006.

Bikhchandani, Sushil, David A. Hirshleifer, and Ivo Welch. "Information Cascades." *The New Palgrave Dictionary of Economics.* London: Palgrave Macmillan/U.K., 2008.

Conway, Brendan. "Investing in Fear Is Big Business." *Wall Street Journal,* November 2010. Retrieved December 12, 2010, from http://online.wsj.com/article/SB1000142405274870 3785704575642643319238142.html

DeBondt, Werner F. M., and Richard Thaler. 1990. "Do Security Analysts Overreact?" *The American Economic Review* (1990).

Dennett, Daniel C. *Darwin's Dangerous Idea.* New York: Simon & Schuster Paperbacks, 1995.

———. *The Intentional Stance.* Boston: MIT Press, 1987.

Epstein, Joshua. "Why Model?" *Journal of Artificial Societies and Social Simulation* (2008).

Forsyth, Richard. "BEAGLE-A Darwinian Approach to Pattern Recognition." *Kybernetes* (1981).

Geist, Richard. *Investor Therapy: A Psychologist and Investing Guru Tells You How to Out-Psych Wall Street.* New York: Crown Business, 2003.

Gigerenzer, Gerd, and Peter M. Todd. *Simple Heuristics that Make Us Smart*. New York: Oxford University Press, 1999.

Goldberg, L. R. "Diganosticians vs. Diagnostic Signs." New York: Psychological Monographs, 1965.

Gould, Stephen Jay, and Niles Eldredge. "Punctuated Equilibria: The Tempo and Mode of Evolution Reconsidered." Baltimore: Paleobiology, 1977.

Grove, W. M., D. H. Zald, A. M. Hallberg, B. Lebow, E. Snitz, and C. Nelson. "Clinical versus mechanical prediction: A meta-analysis." *Psychological Assessment* (2000).

Hall, Alan. "Global Market Perspective." *Elliott Wave International* (2008).

Hardman, David. *Judgment and Decision Making—Psychological Perspectives*. London: British Psychological Society and Blackwell Publishing, Ltd., 2009.

Hens, Thorsten, and Kremena Bachmann. *Behavioural Finance for Private Banking*. Hoboken, NJ: Wiley, 2009.

Holland, John. *Emergence*. New York: Basic Books, 1999.

Holland, John H., and John H. Miller. "Artificial Adaptive Agents in Economic Theory." *The American Economic Review* (1991).

Kahneman, Daniel, and Amos Tversky. "Prospect Theory: An Analysis of Decision Under Risk." *Econometrica* (1979).

Kauffman, Stuart. *At Home in the Universe*. New York: Oxford University Press, 1995.

Kester, Lars. *Quantitative Trading Strategies*. New York: McGraw-Hill, 2003.

Kirman, Alan. "Ants, Rationality, and Recruitment." *The Quarterly Journal of Economics*, vol. 108 (1993).

Langton, Christopher G. "Computation at the edge of chaos." *Physica D* 42 (1990).

Meehl, Paul E. *Clinical versus Statistical Prediction—A Theoretical Analysis and a Review of the Evidence*. Minnesota: The University of Minnesota Press, 1954.

Miller, John, and Scott Page. *Complex Adaptive Systems: An Introduction to Computational Models of Social Life*. New Jersey: Princeton University Press, 2007.

Mitchell, Melanie. *Complexity: A Guided Tour*. New York: Oxford University Press, 2008.

Nickerson, Raymond S. "Confirmation Bias; A Ubiquitous Phenomenon in Many Guises." *Review of General Psychology* (1998).

O'Grada, Cormac, and Morgan Kelly. " Market Contagion: Evidence from the Panics of 1854 and 1857." *American Economic Review* (2000).

Pardo, Robert. *Design, Testing and Optimization of Trading Systems*. Hoboken, NJ: Wiley, 1992.

Parker, Wayne D., and Robert R. Prechter. "Herding: An Interdisciplinary Integrative Review from a Socionomic Perspective." Presentation at the International Conference on Cognitive Economics, Sofia, Bulgaria, 2005.

Peters, Edgar E. *Complexity, Risk, and Financial Markets*. Hoboken, NJ: Wiley, 2001.

Phillips, Joseph. "Towards a Method of Searching a Diverse Theory Space for Scientific Discovery." DS '01 Proceedings of the 4th International Conference on Discovery Science, 2001.

Pinker, Steven. *How the Mind Works*. New York: W.W. Norton & Company, 1997.

Pohl, Rudiger. *Cognitive Illusions: A Handbook on Fallacies and Biases in Thinking, Judgment and Memory*. London: Psychology Press, 2005.

Ponzi, Adam, and Y. Aizawa. "Evolutionary Financial Market Models." *Physica* (2000).

Prechter, Robert R. *At the Crest of the Tidal Wave*. Hoboken, NJ: John Wiley & Sons, 1995.

———. *Prechter's Perspective*. Atlanta: New Classics Library, 1996.

———. "Elliott Wave Theorist." *Elliott Wave International* (2004).

Shiller, Robert J., and John Pound. "Survey Evidence on Diffusion of Interest among Institutional Investors." *Journal of Economics Behavior and Organization* (1986).

Bibliography

Thaler, Richard. *The Winner's Circle.* Princeton: Princeton University Press, 1992.

Tharp, Van K. *Trade Your Way to Financial Freedom.* New York: McGraw-Hill, 2007.

Tversky, Amos, and Daniel Kahneman. "Judgment under Uncertainty: Heuristics and Biases." *Science* (1974).

————. "Extensional versus Intuitive Reasoning: The Conjunction Fallacy in Probability
Judgment." *Psychological Review* (1984).

Waldrop, Mitchell M. *Complexity: The Emerging Science at the Edge of Order and Chaos.*
New York: Simon & Schuster Paperbacks, 1992.

Welsch, Wolfgang. *Rationality and Reason Today.* Edited by Dane R. Gordon and Józef
Niznik. Amsterdam: Criticism and Defense of Rationality in Contemporary Philosophy, 1998.

Zuckerman, Marvin. "Sensation Seeking and risky behavior." *American Psychological Association* xix (2007): 51–72.

INDEX

A

Miller, John, 64, 66, 69, 93
Minnesota Multiphasic Personality
    Inventory (MMPI), 107–108
Mitchell, Melanie, 79–82, 87, 185–189
Modus tollens, 127–128
Money management rules in trading
    systems, 150
Motivational approach, hindsight and, 32
Multi-market test, 204–205
Multiple linear regression analysis (MLR),
    106–107, 199
    See also Linear regression
Myths, market, 111–116

N

Natural Intelligence, 166–169
Neoclassical Economics (NE), flaws of,
    116–119
Neumann, John von, 167
New Concepts in Technical Trading Systems
    (Wilder), 172
A New Kind of Science (Wolfram), 167–168
News media
    attributing causes to trends, 90, 168
    illusory correlation and, 41–42
    simplification bias of, 72, 219–220
    speculation by, 15, 128–129, 135
    trading caused by, 19, 21
Noise-fitting (NF), 203–205
Null hypotheses, 129–131, 152, 196

O

Occam's Razor, 202, 238
Odean, Terrence, 55
O'Grada, Cormac, 84–86
Optimization algorithm, 174

Optimization in problem-solving, 77–78
Optimization programs, 157–158, 191
Options expiration, superstition about, 17
    See also Triple witching days
Origin of Wealth, The (Beinhocker), 119,
    178
Oskamp, Stuart, 35–36
Out-of-sample (OOS) tests, 156–157
Overconfidence bias (OB), 34–36, 43
Over-fitting, 39, 158, 159, 199–200

P

Page, Scott, 64, 93
Parallel terraced scan, 81
Pardo, Robert, 234–235
Parker, Wayne D., 83–84
Parsimony, principle of, 202, 238
Pattern-recognition, 27
Performance measures See Calmar Ratio;
    Sharpe ratio
Personality traits, 20
Peters, Edgar, 60, 71, 78–79, 101
Phillips, Joseph, 169, 170
Pinker, Steven, 160, 161
Political events, market and, 16, 115–116
Ponzi, Adam, 90–91
Popper, Karl, 127
Positive expectancy (PE), 138–141
"Positive Feedbacks in the Economy,"
    121–122
Pound, John, 87
Power law, 93, 94–95
Prechter, Robert, 40–41, 82–84, 103–104,
    111, 117
Predictive modeling See Backtesting
Price mechanism, 118–119
Probability weighting, 54